About the Author

Tony Noble has been a Brighton & Hove Albion supporter since he attended his first game at the Goldstone Ground in 1966. After a couple of seasons spent watching from right at the front of the North Stand at the Goldstone, his family moved away from Hove to North Sussex when he was 12 years old, and Tony has been forced to watch from afar ever since.

Until the 2021-22 season at the grand age of 66, Tony finally has his first ever Brighton season ticket. Over the course of the 2021 -2022 campaign, Tony shared his experiences of what it is like to suddenly be attending Albion games regularly for the first time in half a century.

Preface

I was born at Southlands Hospital in Shoreham by Sea in September 1955 and have my very first memories of Brighton& Hove Albion of course at the Goldstone Ground in Old Shoreham Road. I was lucky enough and it was safe enough in those days that my mum would say to me here is the money to go to watch Brighton and I would catch the number 5 bus from Hangleton near the Grenadier pub and scramble down to the front of the North Stand by the wall and wave my rattle furiously.

So, it was a shock to a young lad who was told by his parents that we all had to move because of my dad's job. That was after the World Cup of 1966, and while I was at Hangleton Junior School with Mr Phillips as our football teacher we went onto win a football medal for the local school team. In our side was the Albion player Roy Jennings's son Richard. What fond memories I have of that period. It was the only football medal I would ever win. Yes, and I still have it!

I never was able to go back to watch the Albion for many reasons until I semi-retired. It was in the last months of Chris Hughton's time as manager that I had my first taste of the Amex Stadium and how wonderful and proud I felt that the club could fight back as they had from near extermination. Following the club closely have elderly parents in a sheltered accommodation a stone's throw from the Withdean Stadium meant that I heard many a roar from there and so wished I could play a part. However, my time came round and now I really relish the chance to visit the stadium at Falmer on home matches.

I find it difficult to visit the away games and so I am always there listening to Johnny cantor and Warren Aspinall as this book will show. I responded to a message in early 2021 from Scott at We Are Brighton.Com who was looking to recruit people to write for the website. I was accepted and that began the series of articles for the 2021-2022 season, 'Thoughts of a 66-year-old first time season ticket holder'.
The reason for putting these articles all together and producing this little book is to tick a box for me and fulfil another boyhood dream of mine of being a journalist / writer. I wanted to work as a journalist while at school however you must pass your exams if you all recall. Well, I failed the lot! All nine O levels and it was not until much later in life that exams and tests became easier for me and by that time I was serving as a firefighter for Kent Fire Rescue and latterly as a Police Officer for Surrey Police as a Detective. I was in fact the first Cybercrime Detective for Surrey Police back in the early 2000's.

So, the book is set up, so you can follow the season from start to finish like a diary and the matches tell of the ups and downs of not just the games themselves but the story behind each one and how I coped keeping up.
I hope you enjoy the read.

ACKNOWLEDGEMENTS

I would like to thank the following people for the help and support in trying to be able to make this a first effort of publishing my own book a reality.

Kristine Susan Noble, my dear wife, who is a true Arsenal supporter as are her family, however the Albion is now her second love, she occupies the seat next to me at every home game.

Scott, from We Are Brighton.Com who gave me my first chance of writing an article and has religiously edited and taught me how to improve my writing style.

Finally, my late mum for letting me go to the Albion as a 10-year-old and enjoy the games at the Goldstone Ground. (Dad was always busy playing football himself for Hove Grammar School Old Boys in Hove Park on a Saturday)

Websites & Watford

August 14th 2021 3pm

Burnley   1 - 2   Brighton

So, the 2021-2022 season is now off to a great start. Burnley last week was a tough team as we knew they would be and that shaky first half, well, just a minor hiccup.

Our team had real determination to fight back, and the boys did so well at Turf Moor to turn the game completely around and ensure it finished Burnley 1-2 Brighton. Up the Albion!

As the week races on towards our first home game of the season at the Amex against Watford this Saturday, I am getting excited. I say to myself: "Hang on Tony you are 66 years old now, not a child"!

Part of the excitement comes from the effort and the determination put in so we can attend games, despite all the restrictions of the previous 18 months. It has been quite amazing.

I cast my mind back on many occasions to the year of 1966. Yes, the year when England last won the World Cup. I was only 11 years old, and I recall with a smile on my face now, being told by my parents that I can go to watch the Albion on my own at that age.

I was armed with a blue and white scarf and my rattle. I would jump on the number five bus and even walk sometimes from Hangleton to the Old Shoreham Road and the Goldstone Ground.

I would go through the turnstiles of the North Stand and get right down the front by the concrete wall behind the goal, ready to cheer on the team of the day.

Well, I still love it just as much now as I did then and that is 55 years later! So good luck lads this Saturday, remember, a positive mental attitude will see you all through and as we know, you never give up as a team.

It is never over till the fat lady sings they used to say! You have proved that at Burnley last weekend already.

The Albion website
I would like to know how everyone is getting on with the Seagulls website? I must admit, it has taken me a while to get to grips with the linking of the various accounts.

I thought I knew about websites and technology, but it has been tough, compounded of course by a recent email sent out in error by the Albion admin team due to a tech issue.

This ended up confusing me even more! Perseverance is the key and having spent several hours in front of the computer, I figured it out eventually.

I am not complaining though as I have been able finally this season make the jump from a My Albion+ Supporter to a fully-fledged season ticket holder.

This of course also causes some confusion, as you sit and say to yourself, "Do I still need a My Albion Membership as well as being a season ticket holder?"

Bless the ticket office staff, they are all so busy on the phone. The waiting time has been over 40 minutes recently on some occasions, so I just hope it sorts itself out.

When you do get to speak to someone on the phone, they are mostly very knowledgeable folk. However, those that are not, do stand out a mile!

Roy Jennings and teammates my boyhood Albion hero

A wonderful start

August 21st 2021 5.30pm

Brighton 2 - 0 Watford

Well, Saturday 21st August 2021 finally arrived. Thousands of us had waited for this day and we all prepared in different ways. Making sure we had our Photo ID plus our Covid vaccination certificates at the ready and a well charged mobile for the season ticket access.

I must say the My Albion 2020 gift we were sent last year of the portable battery phone charger worked a treat. Reading the posts online before I set off to Brighton to watch the Watford game, I think some of us were very sceptical of how the club would cope and deal with all the extra checks required on entry.

The email that was sent out on Friday evening headed 'Pre-Match News' was excellent and the checklist it contained should have helped anyone who was not sure, fully understand their responsibilities. Get used to the new matchday procedure folks – I think it is here to stay for the foreseeable future!

Those working at the turnstiles were very helpful and also quite casual about the actual entry side of the process. However, what did worry me was the huge number of people who had a total disregard for others by not wearing a mask in the public concourses in the stadium and also in the men's toilet areas. An area, of course, we do not want to dwell upon.

Access to the toilets in the East Stand was also a complete shambles. Men were all piling in on top of one another with no order or idea of how many blokes were let in at once. The process should be looked at to protect everyone's health and well-being for future games.

The female toilets all looked very orderly and far more organised – from the outside anyway! That is my moan over and so onto the main point of this week's column… what an afternoon!

Firstly, thank you to Mr Bloom for our flags to wave. An incredible atmosphere, truly one for the history books that we can all look back on and say I was there.

I saw some incredible football played, and once again the determination and the will to win and play great stuff showed through as it had at Burnley. There was a superb 'squad spirit' from the guys.

Like everything in this world, change is a part of our lives that we have to accept and with the advancement of technology these days, we have to be prepared to adapt.

Not many of us know that technology advances extremely quickly. Every calendar year of our lives for example sees technology advance four years in the same time period.

Maybe the fans of the future will have some sort of implant in their arm, showing they are allowed to enter the stadium and there will be no need then for phones then. However, probably not in my lifetime. Let us adapt and be ready for the changes and keep up with tech if we can, it will make our lives much easier as we grow older.

So, working out where my new seat was and what the view would be like was very much part of the early fun, even before the game started.

I had a great view of the pitch, and the only real disappointment of the day was that the Albion's sweetshops had sold out of Wine Gums. I joked and said you have had 18 months to stock up, let us hope they are back in stock for next Saturday!

Being a Neil Diamond fan, it brought the voices into play especially from the North, when the tune rang out around the ground. The feelings of excitement grew, I glanced over to the wall in the North Stand and tried to cast my mind back 55 years and remember.

I felt just as excited at 66 years of age as I did when I was 11 years old at the Goldstone Ground standing by the concrete wall cheering on the team of the day.

The only difference was I was waving an Albion flag on Saturday and not a football rattle, as I did back all those years ago.

When the lads came out of the tunnel onto the pitch, I had goose bumps. It was so good to be back about to watch them play. It felt positive and my god what an amazing start with opportunities within the first thirty seconds.

To see Shane Duffy score as he did was tremendous for the crowd and also for him, I am sure! Once again, he and Yves Bissouma's in my view should both have been men-of-the-match. Bissouma's assist for Neal Maupay in particular was tremendous.

Some readers may well recall a previous goal scorer for the Albion back in the 1960s, Roy Jennings. When Duffy scored with his aerial presence against Watford, the days of gaols from Roy Jennings came flooding back!

I remember Roy Jennings as I went to Hangleton School with his son Richard Jennings. We both played in the school football team and won the school league, which earned us all a medal – the only football trophy I ever won!

Such a wonderful start for the first home game of the season. Roll on another treat of a home game against Everton.

Praise for Johnny and Warren
August 27th 2021 7.45pm

Cardiff 0-2 Brighton   FA CUP Tie

Taking a seat in the lounge at home, tuning in to BBC Radio Sussex and hearing Johnny Cantor and Warren Aspinall give us live commentary from Cardiff City on Tuesday night was as usual up to its great standard.

It is always wonderful to hear them both when you cannot view the game. Two of our Radio Sussex stalwarts providing a service which we are lucky to have. Long may it continue.

Well, we did not have to wait very long for the lounge settee springs to take a real bashing when Jakub Moder scored the Albion's first goal within the first 10 minutes of the game.

Extra loud chanting from the dedicated away supporters could be heard over the airwaves as Moder, according to Warren, made a great run and slotted the ball through the legs of the Cardiff City goalkeeper to put Brighton 1-0 ahead in the first 10 minutes of the game.

I then let my blood pressure regain normality and continued intently listening to Johnny and Warren. Cardiff City may have had streakers invade their pitch, but it was a young Albion side who were streaks ahead of the Bluebirds.

Despite several interruptions on the pitch by Cardiff's well-oiled supporters, some 15 minutes into the second half it was the turn of Andy Zeqiri to score from 14 yards out.

Aptly commentated on by Johnny once again the settee springs took a hammering as I leapt up and down. My wife thought I was having a funny turn!

The commentary said that as the game wore on, a few times Cardiff appeared to have the Albion a little on the back foot. According to Warren, there was a bit of head tennis going on in the last seven minutes of the game inside our penalty box, which was a little worrying as a listener.

I was so hoping captain Jason Steele could keep a clean sheet, which he did. It sounded as if he played a blinder with a very young back four in front of him.

My settee springs could do with a little bit of a rest after the excitement of Cardiff 0-2 Brighton, so thank goodness it is another home game this Saturday against Everton.

Let us hope that the Amex has Wine Gums back in stock, that we can see off Rafa Benitez and his squad and continue with this amazing start to the 2021-22 season.

Scampi and chips but no points
August 28th 2021

Brighton 0 Everton 2

Brighton & Hove Albion have now played four games in total, three in the Premier League and one Carabao Cup match with three wins out of a total of four games. That is a good start to this new season... just think about how poor old Arsenal must be feeling at the moment!

Sitting in the East Stand on Saturday afternoon at the 2-0 defeat to Everton with the sun creeping through on occasions, there was still a thrill in the air.

I am sure all our hopes were high before the game for yet another success. However, it did not quite pan out as well as we all hoped it would.

Rafael Benitez's Everton side appeared much quicker on the break and were faster with their attacking play generally. I think there is some work for Graham Potter to do in that area. However, I am sure he knows what needs to be done.

The two goals that were scored against the Albion by Everton occurred from direct mistakes of the sort that Brighton have not been making in recent weeks.

Also, Robert Sanchez nearly got a hand to that Dominic Calvert-Lewin penalty. If he keeps it out, how different might things have been? Sanchez did really well on Saturday and that is why he was named as the sponsors' man-of-the-match.

I did chuckle when the opposition appeared to be having a little in-house row over who was going to take their penalty. It was like a group of school kids. Benitez obviously has not had the time yet to cover all the bases with his players.

Aside from the football, the best thing to come out of the Everton game was that the Albion Sweet shops had restocked up with Wine Gums. Oh, and nobody was trampled on in the men's toilets.

However, there was still no respect on the concourses for actual mask wearing. With Brighton's high Covid levels at the current time, this matter should really be addressed by the club.

As we left the Upper East Stand it was time to try out the fish and chips outside for the first time. The attendance at the Everton game was higher than the previous week against Watford, it being announced as 30,548, on Saturday afternoon.

This obviously caught out the fish lady who had sold out of fish. I can heartily recommend the scampi and chips having had them instead and they were piping hot as well.

So, while gobbling this lovely post-game scrummy down, it appeared we were standing right by the player's private car park.

The speed with which the players were getting to their cars, well if they had been that fast on the pitch then we may have caught Everton out during the 90 minutes.

You just do not know who you are going to meet at a game. In the queue for the train away from Falmer on Saturday, I got talking with a Liverpool firefighter who was a watch commander in the city.

He was a really nice guy and explained that it is a family thing in Liverpool as to whether you support the blues or the reds. It took him five hours to drive down to the Sussex coast and I heard some supporters saying it had taken them six hours.

They are very dedicated supporters who unfortunately drowned out our North Stand, which was a great shame. We best make more noise against Leicester City in the next home game, me thinks.

We have to wait now for the international break to complete and then see what the Albion can produce when they take on Brentford away on September 11th.

To be seventh in the Premier League at the moment means we could be doing a lot worse, making it strange that there seems to be so much doom and gloom around. Chins up everyone!

Fans' Forum and Faith
September 10th 2021

On Wednesday evening this week, many of you will be aware that it was the Annual Albion Fans' Forum which was broadcast live on BBC Radio Sussex and chaired by commentator Johnny Cantor.

The first question to the panel – which consisted of chairman Tony Bloom, chief Executive Paul Barber, and head coach Graham Potter – got right to the heart of the matter on an issue which has dominated much of the summer transfer window.

It was asked by Tony Parker from Lewes, who is a regular in the North Stand. His question was directed to Potter and after complimenting him on his management, Mr Parker suggested playing Shane Duffy up the front. Potter replied with a smile: "Don't rule it out."

Mr Parker then went onto ask: "There are some fans that feel that we should have signed an established striker this summer. What can you say please to put minds at rest that we are following the perfect path?"

Potter responded diplomatically: "We all want the team to win. It always seems that purchasing an individual would solve the problem. However, that does not always lead to an improvement in the team."

"The most important thing is that the team improves. If I had Neal Maupay, Danny Wellbeck and Leo Trossard sat here tonight, they would say they think they can improve, that they can get better, and there is more to come from them."

"When you have people like that, desperate to do well, desperate to play better, desperate to learn and desperate to improve, I have a responsibility to help them."

"You have to look at how to improve those players. If we can maintain the level we had and then try and add someone to try and help us improve the scoring phase of our game, then yes, we would try and sign that person."

Potter went onto add the easy thing for him would be to sign a striker to keep the fans happy and off his back. He pointed out though that splashing the cash did not necessarily mean we are going to be better as a team or a club.

This was a similar answer to the one that Potter gave when asked about the same issue at the Fans' Forum a year ago. He obviously is very confident in the guys he has and believes that they can get better, solving the problem of not taking enough chances.

Potter did add that at the same time, the club will continue to look in every transfer window for ways to improve the squad. This is reassuring too, and we have seen that this summer with the additions of Enock Mwepu and Marc Cucurella.

For me, it was a very honest, genuine answer that made a lot of sense. And as true Albion fans, we must have faith in our coach and management team – for they have not made many mistakes in getting us into and keeping us in the Premier League.

Over the course of the rest of the evening, there were several very complimentary remarks made to the chairman and the panel. Rightly so, especially after guiding the club through some very difficult months over the past two years.

So, for now, let us get behind the Albion until January when maybe Jesse Lingard will fancy another spell on the Sussex Coast?

Finally, wow, didn't the lads playing in the internationals do well? Jakub Moder, Shane Duffy, and the others are a real credit to Brighton when away representing their nations.

Settee springs take a bashing
September 11th 2021

Brentford 0 Brighton 1

Well, last Saturday afternoon the sun shone on the Brentford Community Stadium as well as on the Albion. For those fans lucky enough to visit the Bees' new ground, there was an added bonus with chairman Tony Bloom right in amongst the Brighton support for the whole match.

Saturday 11th September 2021 was certainly a day to remember in Albion history – as we also remembered the 2,996 people who lost their lives in the twin towers in New York in 20 years ago, including Brighton fan Robert Eaton.

Once again, the game sounded like it got off to a fast start. Listening intently as I do to Johnny Cantor and Warren Aspinall on BBC Radio Sussex, Brighton dominated the first 15 minutes according to the commentators.

This gave the listener great cause for excitement. Then out of the blue, forgive the pun, Ivan Toney the Brentford striker fired a shot from 40 yards out which fortunately went over Robert Sanchez's crossbar. What vision and forethought Toney has?

Shots from distance have been commonplace recently, as evidenced in the game on Sky TV on Monday night between Everton and Burnley when Andros Townsend scored for the Toffees from 25 yards.

What a goal that was! I was just thankful that, unlike Townsend's rocket at Goodison Park, Toney's shot on Saturday flew over the goal. It might have been a different game had it gone in.

Us listeners were informed that Brentford's opportunities in the first were coming from from mistakes that the Albion were making. These mistakes they will surely learn from going forward.

The Bees continued to look the most likely to score as the opening 45 minutes wore on. Toney for Brentford got another shot away and luckily, for the second time, over the crossbar it went.

It was soon after that the commentators reported that Adam Webster had suffered a groin injury and had to come off. This allowed Graham Potter to substitute Webster with Jacob Moder. Straight away Moder was reported as "driving on up the pitch".

Adam Lallana then took a ball straight in the face, which seemed to stop a session of football ping pong and allowed play to steady down. The restart resulted in a drop ball.

So the first half came to a close at 0-0 and to be fair it was lucky the Albion were not 2-0 down, especially when Brentford missed their best chance of the game in time added on. All the quality so far appeared to come from Brentford with Brighton sounding very scrappy on the radio.

Things improved in the second half, particularly for Leandro Trossard who was playing a blinder. It sounded like he was involved in most of the action and that if one team were going to score in the final 20 minutes, it would be the Albion.

As the game got closer to the full-time whistle, the more nervous I became. Could Brighton find a way to make a breakthrough? We all know that feeling, I am sure.

Then in the 90th minute, Trossard seized the opportunity and curved one into the right-hand corner. I jumped for joy, forgetting I was sitting on the settee. The lampstand took a fall, but who cares as it finished Brentford 0-1 Brighton.

What an exciting ending, even for a radio listener. What it must have been like amongst the Albion supporters actually present I don't know... perhaps Mr Bloom will tell us!

Who pulled the plug on the 66-year-old season ticket holders My Albion TV?
September 18th 2021

Brighton 2 Leicester 1

Now it was a slightly different experience for this 66-year-old season ticket holder when it came to Brighton v Leicester City.

It is our timeshare week in Madeira and, having missed out on last year's visit because of obvious reasons, the wife and I have jetted off to Portugal to enjoy some sunshine.

Which meant missing the vital home game against the Foxes. Was there a way around this? Well, I thought to myself, I can install a VPN (virtual private network) application and tune into My Albion TV through the Albion website.

This allowed me to listen to Johnny Cantor and Warren Aspinall's commentary on BBC Radio Sussex, and so there I found myself on Sunday afternoon, sitting ready for the game in the shade with a nice cool drink.

Unlike whilst listening to Brentford 0-1 Brighton a week earlier, there were no settee springs to damage thank goodness; I just had to be a little careful with the apartment furniture.

Leicester was Brighton's fifth game of the Premier League season with three of the previous four already won.

It seems to me that the national press is not quite sure what to make of us so far as, despite the flying start, they are still not giving many column inches to the Albion. We will have to put this down to it being early days yet, as Graham Potter quite rightly points out.

There was of course sad news earlier in the day of the loss of a football titan Jimmy Greaves, and the club paid their respects to him with a tribute before kick-off.

Once Greaves had received the applause his life and career deserved, I heard the roar of the crowd in the background of the broadcast.

In an instant, I wished I was at the game like all supporters would. The singing in the North Stand to start with could be heard behind Johnny and Warren.

I still think we can sing louder than that though – and we must make plenty of noise to cheer the team on as the weeks drift by and the games become tougher.

The commentators described the Amex pitch as being like a carpet. Warren Aspinall commented: "If you can't play football on this Johnny, you can't play football anywhere."

I listened intently, so pleased that I could at least hear the commentary from over one thousand miles away even if I could not see the game.

In the first six minutes, it sounded like the Albion had limited possession and were struggling somewhat. The nerves started to build as the feeling from the commentary was that Leicester City had all the play.

When Johnny then said that the Albion had started to come to life, I felt a sigh of relief. Central to that appeared to be Marc Cucurella who was making a big impact on his first home game for the Albion.

He could be heard over the airwaves doing his best to create chances and opportunities. One of those came from Robert Sanchez claiming a Leicester corner and launching a counter attack.

Cucurella took control of the ball direct from his goalkeeper and then fed Neil Maupay, leading to a shot and a Brighton corner. The resulting corner found Shane Duffy whose header was unluckily wide.

Shortly after this there was excitement as Solly March had the opportunity to take a first time shot. Instead, he took an extra touch, and the chance went begging, much to Warren's anguish.

Adam Lallana was next to be wasteful on the 30-minute mark when he hit a shot which was described as flying into the South Stand. That one made me spill my drink.

I sat there wondering if we were going to grab the game by the scruff of the neck or if this would be a return to last season of not making the most of dominating.

We had at least settled into the game after that strong Leicester start, something which Warren confirmed. Warren also continued to gush with praise about Cucurella, so it was no surprise when Cucurella ended up being the sponsor's man of the match.

With half time approaching, Shane Duffy put a really good header on target which needed the arm of Jannik Vestergaard to keep it out. Neal Maupay struck a confident penalty past Kasper Schmeichel, sending the Leicester goalkeeper the wrong way.

Watching the highlights back, there was plenty of gamesmanship going on from Schmeichel before the penalty could be taken. Maupay did well to not let this deter him in any way.

There was a deep sigh and concern all round when the commentators reported that Yves Bissouma had gone down with a knock on the rear of his knee.

With a hobbling Bissouma and seven minutes of the first half to see out, I began crossing my fingers, biting my nails and praying that we could keep concentration and make it to the break with the lead intact.

And then... someone pulled the plug out of My Albion TV. Johnny and Warren's commentary was gone, the last noise heard sounding like a large amplifier being unplugged followed by a partial male voice and then nothing.

What is going on I thought? You cannot seriously tell me this has happened just before half time. I grabbed my mobile and pulled up My Albion TV on that. Once again, dead with nothing coming through.

Next, I took the tried and tested approach of switching everything off and back on again. Still nothing. I tried connecting to the Albion website via 4G rather than Wi-Fi to see if the internet was at fault. That did not work either.

By this point, I was tearing my hair out. It must be half time by now and although I had no idea if we were still winning, surely somebody would realise the plug had been pulled out once the action stopped for 15 minutes.

I then decided to try and call the club. I suspected this would be a waste of time and so it proved as the recorded voice gave no option of anyone to speak to.

With all options exhausted and the commentary not coming back, I was left with no choice but to spend the second half constantly refreshing the live blog on the Albion website. It turns out this is a stressful way to follow a game.

Suddenly, there was an explosion of news five minutes into the second half. Solly March had been brought down by Ryan Bertrand on the right-hand side, Leandro Trossard sent a free kick over and Danny Welbeck headed home.

The problem with the live blog is that it hardly updates. This left me very twitchy until the next update came through with 61 minutes played, revealing that Jamie Vardy had pulled one back.

Staring at the screen waiting for it update again, I was left fearing the worst about what the next sentence would say when it appeared. Would we be on the end of another unlucky decision like those of last year that went against the Albion?

Next, the blog told us that March had been replaced by Enock Mwepu. My thought process told me this was Potter beginning to think about shoring up the defence to try and see out the game.

Reading that Leicester had two goals disallowed for offside – both correctly in my opinion after watching back – and that Big Dan Burn had come on for Welbeck confirmed that we must be under pressure.

When the blog said there were five added minutes, I did not know what to do with myself. When it then updated to confirm a final score of Brighton 2-1 Leicester, it became clear that a great team effort had delivered three points.

Hopefully, they get My Albion TV up and running again for the Swansea game as my nerves cannot take another game being updated through the live blog.

Finally, a word of warning if you are a new season ticket holder like me and are not fully aware how the ticket exchange works. I put our two season tickets up for resale as I knew we would be away for the Leicester game, thinking they would appear for another supporter to buy.

This is the not how resale works though, apparently. The ground has to completely sell out before the ticket exchange is open and your seat appears for sale. With tickets still available, there was no chance for us to sell our seats to another fan.

How to listen to a Brighton game in a restaurant without your wife noticing
September 22nd 2021

Brighton 2   Swansea 0

The lengths we go to when it comes to listening or watching the Albion! It was mid-afternoon in Madeira and with Brighton set to take on Swansea City in the League Cup, I had to start planning how I was going to keep up to date with the game. The problem? I was having to tow the line and go out to dinner with my wife and two friends.

This meant that a stable My Albion TV connection and tuning into Johnny Cantor and Warren Aspinall to hear all the action as it happened live was not on the cards.

Of course, on Sunday afternoon it had not been on the cards for the 2-1 win over Leicester City either. You may remember that I lost connection after 39 minutes and never got it back, causing a frantic second half spent trying to keep up on a live blog.

Presuming there were no such technology issues this time, I found myself coming up with a way to covertly listen. I made sure that the Norton App on my phone allowed me to have the VPN activated here in Madeira.

I then tuned into My Albion TV, which was working okay. So far, so good. Could I get away with listening at the table? This was the big question. It was booked for 7.30pm, the exact same time that the game would be kicking off at the Amex.

I tuned in just after 7pm and Johnny and Warren came through loud and clear using a very stable signal from the Hotel Wi-Fi. I really enjoyed the Glenn Murray piece and will be listening to the full podcast later.

As I walked through the hotel, still all good, the signal was loud and clear. I then moved across the road to the restaurant and switched to 4G. The signal remained strong.

To ensure I was able to get away with my plan, I had to ensure that nobody knew I was listening. Part of this involved carrying on conversation as normal with my wife and friends, something which I was surprisingly adept at.

One of our friends said to me: "I didn't realise you had to wear a hearing aid now?!" They had mistaken the Samsung Galaxy Pod in my left ear for a hearing aid. This was perfect. "Only on occasions," I replied whilst chucking to myself.

The undercover operation was going well at this point. Being a bit of a gadget freak, I also wear a Samsung Galaxy watch. I felt myself in the first few minutes feeling a little tense as the play did not sound as if it was going the Albion's way.

Johnny and Warren's commentary was excellent as normal, even though there did not seem much to get excited about. I must have grunted or winced a few times when Swansea got close to Jason Steele's goal as my friends asked me if I was okay. "Bad indigestion" was my answer.

What I was not ready for was an alert from my watch, bleeping very loudly. It was a notification from BBC Sport saying that Aaron Connolly had just scored the first Brighton goal.

Strange, as Johnny was telling me that Steve Alzate had the ball in a harmless position. Eventually, the delayed My Albion TV signal caught up and Alzate and Alexis Mac Allister had worked the ball out to Connolly on the left. He shot, it took a slight deflection off a Swansea defender and ended up in the back of the net.

A combination of the watch notification and my loud amazement at Brighton taking the lead suddenly alerted my wife and our two friends to the fact that I was listening to Brighton v Swansea and not wearing a new hearing aid. I was over the moon with the 1-0 lead and remonstrated that fact to my table and the rest of the restaurant.

Aaron Connolly's second goal five minutes later was once again announced by my watch. This time, I had a little punch of the air which narrowly missed a passing waiter, as I was later informed by my wife.

Who cared though? Brighton were 2-0 ahead before half time against a good Championship side. I kept the commentary going right up to the end of the game and was so happy as a fan that I could follow all the way through.

I was proud of the young team for working so hard and having the true determination and confidence that they can win and also perform well.

With a final score of Brighton 2-0 Swansea, a place in the fourth round and a great sirloin steak, who could ask for a better evening out?

Seeing the Amex from the air before Maupay sent us sky high
September 25th 2021

Crystal Palace 1   Brighton 1

Monday 27th September 2021 is a day that will be remembered in infamy! Brighton secured a 1-1 draw at Selhurst Park and unlike the previous two matches, I was able to watch it all unfold as my holiday came to an end. What a homecoming.

My journey began at 6am in Funchal in Madeira, Portugal. If all went 100 percent smoothly, then I would be back home and tuned into MNF on Sky Sports by the time Palace and the Albion were set to do battle.

Whilst eating my breakfast I checked the Flight Radar App and took a deep breath as I could see the outbound EasyJet flight had left Gatwick on time.

This was the main hurdle to jump. Had this outbound flight been delayed, then we would have been delayed leaving Madeira. That our plane was out of Gatwick when it should have been made the journey a lot less stressful.

The exercise of filling out extra paperwork, taking Covid-19 tests and putting information into passenger locator forms would next be put to the test.

Thankfully, this went like clockwork. Everyone on the flight got through the necessary checks in a timely manner, there were no delays and we landed back in England at 3.45pm having soared over the Amex on route. That felt like an omen for a successful night ahead.

After sailing through the eGates, we were back home to Crawley Down within an hour. The dog was picked up, we unpacked, had glorious fish and chips and finally, I took my place in front of the television for a nail-biting evening.

Nail biting it might have been, but at least there was no need to keep refreshing a live blog every 30 seconds on my phone like the Leicester game after somebody pulled the plug on My Albion TV.

Or have to try and listen unnoticed to radio commentary whilst having dinner at a restaurant with my wife and two friends like for the Swansea match. Two experiences I would rather not go through again.

I must say, I was very worried when I saw the players' faces as they walked out the tunnel. I thought they all looked quite worried... but then it must be very daunting to have thousands of Palace fans booing you.

It was very nervy to watch, so much so that I had to change my seat from the settee as the springs cannot stand any further damage from overexcited reactions.

With the heavy pressing by Palace, it looked as if we might concede a goal in the first half. Then as the clock ran up to half time, I thought we were would safely make it in on level terms.

Nobody was going to do a Joel Veltman against Everton, were they? Wrong, Leandro Trossard did exactly that to take out Conor Gallager and that was it.

I never thought that Wilfried Zaha would miss the opportunity, even though I have so much faith in Robert Sanchez. I would have given big odds-on Sanchez saving a shot had Gallagher got one away rather than be fouled and that was what made conceding a penalty disappointing.

The scene was now set for an interesting second half, during which Graham Potter made three changes to try and get a response. It was fairly obvious who the one player we needed was. Get well soon please, Yves!

Like all of us, I thought it was over and we had lost it as the game reached injury time. Never mind, or tant pis as they say in France.

Talking of the French, it was at that moment that our little Neal Diamond appeared. Maupay displayed the most incredible touch to lift the ball into the Palace goal in a game which, any other time, we would have lost. Crystal Palace 1-1 Brighton, amazing.

It just goes to prove, as I have always been taught as a retired professional sportsman, that it is never over until the fat lady sings.

The Albion refused to give up and as we have seen so many times already this season, there is a sure determination to win through the day.

No, this may not have been a win and Brighton certainly did not play their best. But as Adam Lallana said in his interview on the Albion website, you cannot always be at your best.

The players now have a chance to rest up and train hard towards the end of the week, ready to show Arsenal exactly what Brighton are made of.

Seagulls may specialise in pinching things at the last minute and that is a trait the Albion have at the minute, but for the sake of our blood pressures I hope we score early – and I suspect one goal may not be enough…

Singing in the rain: A family feud for this 66-year-old season ticket holder
October 2nd 2021

Brighton 0 Arsenal 0

Well, what an evening that was at the Amex. It was terrific to watch Brighton do battle with Arsenal as the wind sped at gusts reportedly as high as 65mph and swirling rain came down like stair rods. Proper football weather, some might say.

This is an exciting fixture in our family as the wife's side are – and always will be – staunch Arsenal followers. My wife, her late father who was born in 1915, and his father before him were all Arsenal fans.

We do not have a detailed family history, but it is safe to assume that her granddad would have been there right back when the Gunners joined the Football League in 1893. With this in mind, I had to watch what I said in the lead up to the game.

There were other slight complications whilst getting ready for the fixture. Our dear little puppy had to have an operation three days before the game, so we needed to find someone to nurse him whilst we were at the Amex.

Once that was in place, rainwear was donned, and we set off. Not that rainwear was much good; we still ended up absolutely drowned going from our car to catch the train, then even wetter from Falmer Station to the East Stand Upper entrance.

I thought twice about buying a programme from my usual spot on the way up the hill, knowing it would be nothing more than papier-mache by the time we got into the ground.

My first stop on entering the East Upper is always the gents. As I walked in this time, I was confronted with several young men carrying out what looked like some sort of ballet moves up against the wall in the toilet.

After I did what I intended to do in the gents, I looked over my shoulder intrigued and continued to see these young men hopping on one leg and using the wall for support.

Then all became clear. Every 30 seconds, they would use their spare hand to hit the wall hand dryer whilst their other handheld up their leg. They were drying their trousers having been soaked by the rain.

"Great idea guys", I said to them as I left. I did not mention that they appeared to be ballet dancing however, thinking that may not have gone down too well.

Now with a programme, the biggest hot dog I have had in a long while and the famous Albion wine gums, it was off to take a pew in a stadium where the wind was swirling like a tornado.

Despite the rain, the pitch looked absolutely fantastic. Much credit should go to the Albion ground staff for the superb work they do on the playing surface.

I always love the pre-game hoe down and get into the music being played. There was a notable absentee this week though.

Why did we did not hear Neil Diamond singing Sweet Caroline? Perhaps the intellectual property rights have caught up with the club? Will we have to wait, and see?

A few Arsenal players popped their heads out from the tunnel early on, thought better of it and jogged back inside. I must say I did not blame them.

The first brave guys from the Albion to warm up were, as usual, our three goalkeepers led by Robert Sanchez. It was interesting to watch him place long kicks down the pitch whilst warming up, taking the wind drift into account. He was so accurate.

Before the game started there was a sign of respect and appreciation paid to the late Roger Hunt, who passed away very recently. He was of course a Liverpool great amongst others and a member of Sir Alf Ramsey's 1966 World Cup Squad.

It was clear the Arsenal fans were in terrific voice and were making more noise than the North Stand. When you sit at the side of the pitch, you can get a good idea where most of the noise is coming from.

I think we can all do better on the atmosphere front, even if it did improve once the game kicked off and the North began to liven up.

Our family tension was livening up too as John Moss prepared to blow his whistle for kick-off. Not daring to show her true colours thank goodness, my dear wife sat there quite quietly with her hood up, mask on and scared to look as the Albion applied pressure to the Gunners.

Leandro Trossard took a heavy tumble as early as the third minute, just outside the Arsenal 18-yard-box at the south end of the ground. Mr Moss eventually stopped play so Trossard could be treated.

The Albion appeared more determined than normal to get ahead with at least half a dozen good chances in the first half. None of those could put Brighton forward though.

Instead, we were left to raise a smile when Arsenal was awarded a free kick in the middle of the pitch with around 29 minutes played.

Neal Maupay spotted that Mr Moss had dropped his tin of white spray used to mark where the ball should be placed, or a wall should stand.

Maupay duly picked it up and marked the ground where Arsenal's free kick should be taken, unbeknown to the referee. When he then handed the tin back to Mr Moss, he had one of his great smiles on his face. Despite the howling gales and swirling rain, Maupay was at least enjoying himself out there.

Halfway was reached and as we know it was 0-0. Nobody had managed to put the ball in the onion bag, to coin a phrase used on a weekly basis by BBC Sussex commentator Warren Aspinall.

The second half seemed to really fly by. The Albion players, for me, were outstanding. To single out a couple, man-of-the-match Marc Cucurella showed fantastic potential and skill.

Shane Duffy again and Lewis Dunk made us look strong at the back and dangerous from set pieces, especially Duffy who had a couple of headers narrowly miss. Dan Burn did so well keeping Bukayo Saka under control, even if Burn could not outrun the England international.

Arsenal had a couple of chances in the second half, the most memorable of which came when Pierre-Emerick Aubameyang went around Robert Sanchez.

Duffy though played a blinder. He was not to know that the offside flag was going to be raised, producing a great tackle to prevent Aubameyang doing what he does best in an opponent's goalmouth.

Amongst those players who missed chances over the 90 minutes for Brighton were Trossard, Maupay, Cucurella, Burn, Adam Lallana and Dunk and Duffy as already mentioned.

Even though it finished Brighton 0-0 Arsenal, it was such an exciting game to watch as an Albion supporter. Not so much my other half, who had her head in her hands on several occasions.

She even said at one point, "My granddad would turn in his grave if he was watching this performance from Arsenal.

Thankfully, the rain stopped as the full-time whistle blew and queuing for a train home became easier to cope with. And at least those of us waiting to leave Falmer were doing so with a full set of teeth.

According to the Adrian Kajumba of the Daily Mail, Arsenal defender Gabriel reappeared on the Amex pitch long after the final whistle to search the penalty area for a tooth he had lost during this game.

Not only was this not the first time this had happened to poor Gabriel, but the previous occasion was also when he played against Brighton apparently. Let us hope he can get into a dentist this week, unlike many of the population!

Below par at Norwich, but there are no easy games in the Premier League
October 16th 2021

Norwich 0 Brighton 0

Saturday arrived and according to the weather forecast, the sun was shining on Carrow Road. Whilst Brighton prepared themselves to take on Norwich City, I had to ensure that the AA batteries were in top form and ready to load into the Roberts DAB Radio.

Listening via radio means hearing our trusted BBC Radio Sussex commentators Johnny and Warren in real-time. Listening via My Albion TV means a time delay issue so that you get BBC notifications saying we have scored before the commentary tells you.

Something I was by now fed up with having experienced it whilst trying to follow from holiday in Portugal last month.

Goal notifications were not really relevant on this occasion as it finished Norwich 0-0 Brighton. Over the airwaves, it sounded as if the Canaries were going to run us off the road in Norfolk, the home of Lotus cars.

It was a frustrating listen and only the sterling work of Dan Burn, Lewis Dunk and Shane Duffy saved me from hurling the radio down the garden in frustration. I am not an angry man; however I do get very emotional when it comes to the Albion and the beautiful game.

Such a below par performance from Brighton did not help. Chances were few and far between, although it was disappointing that the tackle on Neal Maupay by Tim Krul did not see a penalty given in our favour as that may well have changed the whole outlook of the game.

Leandro Trossard too came close, hitting the bar with a shot which if Krul did not get a fingertip onto, would have been a cracking goal.

We were though more indebted to those lads at the back and Robert Sanchez who were in top form to claim a clean sheet.

Brighton head coach Graham Potter says each week in his press conference that every team and every game in the Premier League is tough.

Just because Norwich were at the bottom of the table, it did not necessarily mean an easy game for the Seagulls. And he is right, isn't he?

Brighton have been superb for most of the season and if the guys keep up the great work, it will continue to pay off.

I am really looking forward to getting back to the Amex this Saturday for the home game against Manchester City – will Pep Guardiola be as grumpy with Potter as he was when leaving the playing surface, the last time the two men met back in May?

Our trusted head coach really is this squad's GP, as it says on his tracksuit. He will be guiding the players this week on the training field and in the classroom, giving them a real 'Pep' talk (apologies for the pun).

That will focus on how to beat City. Us fans have a part to play too and must not get downhearted if things do not go our way. We have to shout the loudest, cheer on the team and give them all the enthusiasm and help we can.

With players coming back from injury, this great start to the season we are all thankful for could get even better. The positive approach of the squad has been amazing and fed into to some really good performances, mixed with a bit of luck of course.

Brighton are not dissimilar to Brentford right now. The sheer determination the Bees showed against Chelsea was equally amazing – a great game to catch up on that if you have not seen it yet.

Just like the Albion, Brentford have made a flying start to the season. They never know when to give up and as we all know, it is never over until the fat lady sings.

Let us hope she is singing on three points and another famous victory over the champions. Up the Albion!

Kevin was nobody's friend – unlike Grealish who made a young fan's day
October 23rd 2021

Brighton 1 Man City 4

Positives from Brighton v Manchester City – it was not raining as hard for this home fixture as it had in the previous game at the Amex against Arsenal.

Although we had been successful against City last season, deep down I think most of us did not expect the Albion to be winners this time around. It would all depend on the number of errors made.

Whereas Norwich the week before were not able to major on Brighton mistakes, the champions ruthlessly exposed them, and their reward was a comfortable looking final score of Brighton 1-4 Manchester City.

I must say that the effort and determination to fight on despite the three-goal deficit at the start of the second half was brilliant.

The highlight of the 90 minutes for me though came in the first half and that goal line overhead kick to clear the ball away by Lewis Dunk – absolutely incredible timing.

Sitting in the East Stand Upper, several of the decisions made by referee Kevin Friend were very clearly incorrect and because of that, you kind of got the feeling that nothing was going to go right for the Albion.

When you are parallel to the North Stand goal line, the ball goes out of play and it is quite clearly an Albion corner, well, you can understand the anger and frustration of fans when Mr Friend awards a throw.

Aside from the referee, I really enjoyed the game. You never feel confident of winning against one of the best squads in the world, but Brighton managed to match City in that second half. When a team that good start time wasting, you know you have them on the back foot.

Brighton were much improved once Tariq Lamptey and Enock Mwepu were on the pitch. Lamptey produced that moment of magic against Jack Grealish right in front of me and yet I still had to watch it back several times on TV to believe it had happened.

For Lamptey to go swerving, ducking, and diving around a player like Grealish just goes to show the talent we have under our bonnet.

Speaking of Grealish, he showed what a great guy he is before the game when taking time to speak to a young fan in the East Stand during the City warm up.

Gully and Sally on the touchline managed to attract Grealish's attention, pointing to a supporter who clearly wanted to meet the England superstar.

Over Grealish came, giving the little boy a day and memory, which will last a lifetime. What a fantastic gesture when most Premier League footballers would have simply continued warming up.

It was a disappointment when City added their fourth late on and I do not think that they deserved to win by three.

Nobody could deny that it was a great game to watch, and the Albion remained in fourth spot in the Premier League as we left the Amex on Saturday night.

Finally, City's supporters were in really good voice, out singing the North Stand. Next time out against Newcastle United, we need to be cheering the Albion on from all three sides of the pitch.

Kevin went from enemy against City to Friend at Liverpool

October 30th 2021

Liverpool 2 Brighton 2

Saturday afternoon arrived and once again it was BBC Radio Sussex that gave us the commentary on the game between Liverpool and Brighton at Anfield.

I am sure the more technical of us were able to find time to search for an overseas streaming channel. However, I cannot condone this as it is not a lawful broadcast in the UK.

From the commentators' input we all tried to picture the scene of an autumnal afternoon with some sunshine on Merseyside. I don't know about you, but I wasn't quite sure what to think about this game.

I am beginning to find myself getting nervous in matches against the very, very top teams, like Manchester City last week. Of course, we are a top team this year, but I am sure some of you will know what I mean.

With the 3pm kick off and batteries checked for the radio, we were off and running. Listeners did not have long to wait for some action, as early doors Leandro Trossard just failed to beat Alisson in the opening few minutes.

Just as you started to think, come on lads, this sounds better than the City game, Jordan Henderson slotted one home to put Liverpool 1-0 up.

Warren Aspinall was upset, not with the goal but that his TV monitor at the ground in the commentary spot had packed up. Johnny Cantor did not have one either, so neither of them could not see the replay.

When I saw it on BBC Match of The Day it looked as if Robert Sanchez was wearing deep sea divers' boots, bless him, as he never moved! It was so quick and that is why Liverpool are one of the best teams in the world.

Shortly after, our returning star Yves Bissouma narrowly missed slotting it home in the Liverpool net as he hit the right-hand post of Alisson's goal. So close from Yves – I love it when he has a go from distance.

Being 1-0 down and really not quite settling into the game, of course the next deadly blow came from Sadio Mane who headed past Robert Sanchez to make it 2-0 to Liverpool – and all before we had played even 25 minutes.

That is when we probably all thought, here we go again! Brighton though rallied and our rising prodigy Enoch Mwepu headed over the bar in another near miss for the Albion, so perhaps we were not completely out of it.

The next goal would be crucial and so I turned the volume on the radio up as it was getting exciting. Then like an arrow to the heart, Mane put the ball in the Albion net, and it looked like we were 3-0 down and all before half time. Manchester City all over again, I thought to myself.

Oh, ye of little faith! Warren commented straight away: "We are not playing netball or basketball are we Johnny, that's handball."

The VAR official watching on from Stockley Park for the game against Liverpool was – believe it or not – last week's referee, Kevin Friend.

Mr Friend was certainly not the Albion's friend against Manchester City when he officiated that game. He reviewed the Mane goal and ruled that it had struck the Liverpool forward's hand. This time, Kevin was Brighton's friend and the score remained Liverpool 2-0 Albion.

Now Brighton had to make the most of that reprieve. I heard the excitement in Johnny's voice as a promising move began to build.

Solly March slid the ball to Mwepu, who went for goal with a magnificent strike which dropped just behind Allison, under the crossbar and into the net. A world class goal to make it Liverpool 2-1 Brighton. Game on.

We were reminded how close to half time Mwepu had struck when the deepest Liverpudlian voice you have ever heard appeared in the background of the broadcast, telling the spectators in the ground that there were two minutes of added time. Warren Aspinall thought it was a Halloween character on the end of the stadium PA!

There was light at the end of the tunnel for the Albion as they went in for the break only one goal behind when, without Mr Friend, it could have been three.

It was time to take a breath and stick the kettle on. As much as I love BBC Radio Sussex, I really miss not seeing the action live and person.

At the start of the second half, the question was which team were going to make the first impact? It looked like Mo Salah, but his great play and goal was flagged offside.

Some tidy footwork from the Albion and a clever back hell to Adam Lallana saw the ex-Liverpool man get a shot on target but it was repelled by Alisson.

Brighton were now coming onto the front foot. An amazing pass by Sanchez started an Albion attack, finding Cucurella. He slid it into Lallana, who fed Trossard to shoot and make it Liverpool 2-2 Brighton at Anfield.

The determination and grit these guys have to fight back from 2-0 down against one of the best teams in the world is quite amazing. And what a strike from Trossard.

Brighton might even have gone onto win. There was a further great chance from Mwepu who narrowly missed slotting home when denied by a good save from Alisson.

Substitute Tariq Lamptey then showed what he was made of and beat several Liverpool players before setting up Trossard. The Belgian again put his effort past Alisson, only to be caught slightly offside.

So, the game as we all know gave us a very well-deserved point. It was a truly excellent performance by the Albion given the circumstances which the opening 25 minutes left us in.

As I write this now, we are in eighth place in the Premier League after 10 games. Roll on Saturday when a winless Newcastle United come to the Amex.

It would be a mistake to think of that as a guaranteed three points, however. We should never lose sight of what Graham Potter constantly tells us – that there are no easy games in the Premier League. Up The Albion.

A wonderful Remembrance tribute – and then Sanchez saved the day
November 6th 2021

Brighton 1 Newcastle 1

Brighton & Hove Albion are very good at lots of things but one area they excel in is paying respect when pre-game tributes are required at the Amex.

With the Newcastle game being our final home fixture before Remembrance Sunday, the club appropriately remembered all the fallen heroes from previous world wars and conflicts.

The Albion management team deserve a lot of credit for going streets ahead of many other clubs with their wonderful montage of poppies displayed in the East Stand.

Every spectator on that side of the ground played a part – including myself – by holding up their relevant piece of card prior to the two-minute silence.

The Surrey & Sussex Drum & Bugle Corp played the Last Post to a silent crowd. It was a reminder to us all that there are more important things in life than football… and then the game kicked off and a lot of us seemed to forget!

Whereas many seemed to be expecting three points based on Newcastle being at the other end of the table, I arrived at the Amex thinking otherwise.

As Graham Potter always says, there are no easy games in the Premier League – even if on paper, it looked like our team should have walked it against a Magpies side who came to Brighton winless.

They left winless too, all thanks to Robert Sanchez. Had the Albion goalkeeper not taken the drastic action he did in the final minutes, then we would have lost the game 2-1.

Not that it seemed like that at the time. My thoughts were "Blimey, what's going on here?" when Sanchez charged from goal and tripped Callum Wilson. On later reflection, I realised what a good decision he had made.

It meant that Newcastle left the Amex with only five points on the board and marooned in the relegation zone. Eddie Howe of course was sitting in the director's box, watching and scrutinising every move I am sure before taking over on Monday.

My worry that this would not be a straightforward 90 minutes left me really quite nervous at the start. Lewis Dunk lost the toss and Newcastle turned us around, meaning that Brighton attacked the North Stand in the first half. That has not happened for a very long time and perhaps it contributed to a slow start from the Albion.

Brighton began to settle as the game reached the 20-minute mark. The moment then arrived when Leandro Trossard used his nifty moves to set up a shot inside the penalty area. Contact came from Newcastle defender Ciaran Clark, but referee David Coote said no penalty.

VAR at Stockley Park took an age to review the decision and then asked Mr Coote to have another look on the pitch side monitor. It was heart-in-mouth time and Mr Coote did not help, taking even longer than VAR had to watch the replay back.

Eventually, he turned back to the North Stand, signalled in the air the sign for a VAR decision, and pointed to the penalty spot. The North Stand erupted and for the only time all evening, shut down the very loud Toon Army.

It was the Newcastle fans who dominated the atmosphere throughout, something that we really must address. The North Stand needs to turn the noise levels up to give the team every bit of encouragement they can, especially in games against stubborn opponents like Newcastle.

Despite this very long wait from foul to penalty, Trossard kept his cool and put a great effort past Karl Darlow to give Brighton the lead.

Now we needed to find the killer second as everyone knew that if Miguel Almirón or Allan Saint-Maximin were given an opportunity, then they had the quality to hurt the Albion.

That second never arrived. The closest it came was when Sanchez started a move with a pinpoint pass to Marc Cucurella.

It seems sometimes like Sanchez has some sort of homing beacon in his boots with the perfect accuracy he displays in putting the ball to an exact spot 60 yards away.

Moments like that show what an amazing goalkeeper Sanchez is – and it is better to remember those than the mistakes because when a goalkeeper has a bad day, it really shows up compared to an outfield player.

Once Cucurella had possession from Sanchez, he found Adam Lallana who shot wide. I am positive that one of these weeks, Lallana will slot one home rather than the wrong side of the post!

Then of course came the Newcastle equaliser from Isaac Hayden, which did not bode well for the Albion. Despite plenty of effort, we seemed to struggle after that and the problems nearly peaked when the game reached stoppage time.

An Albion attack broke down, Joel Linton slid through a long ball which Shane Duffy could not cut out and that left Wilson with only Sanchez to beat.

Sanchez advanced, the two came together and Wilson went to ground. Mr Coote looked at the replay again which showed Sanchez had clipped the right ankle of Wilson and so the Brighton goalkeeper was shown a red card for denying a goal scoring opportunity.

There were still four minutes of seven left to play. Lewis Dunk donned the oversized goalkeeper shirt and gloves, and I took a big gulp. I was sure that if Newcastle had a single shot on target, they would win.

They had that opportunity with a direct free kick in a good position with seconds remaining. To my absolute amazement, Jonjo Shelvey opted to put the ball out to the right-hand touchline rather than have a crack on Dunk's goal. A terrible piece of decision making which, along with Sanchez taking one for the team, saved the day.

Despite the disappointment of not beating Newcastle, we move into the international break with Brighton seventh in the Premier League having accumulated 17 points from 11 games so far. That is testament to the great squad and coaching staff we currently have at the Albion.

Aston Villa away is up next, a tough enough game even without Villa's players and fans wanting to impress new boss Steven Gerrard in his first match in charge – similar to Newcastle and the watching Howe.

Another reminder – and I am sure Graham will tell us in the lead up to the Villa Park trip – that there are no easy games in the Premier League…

Don't be too disappointed by Brighton falling to the new manager bounce
November 20th 2021

Aston Villa 2 Brighton 0

There were a lot of downhearted Brighton fans out there following the Albion's 2-0 defeat at Aston Villa on Saturday and it was very sad to see so many terrible comments pop up on some social media sites.

The sacking of Dean Smith meant that the game already featured a tremendous amount of hype in the media as Villa looked to shake their five-game losing streak. When Steven Gerrard then signed on the dotted line, the hype went into overdrive really.

For 83 minutes, the Albion did well against a Villa side containing the likes of Ollie Watkins and Danny Ings. When you have strikers that good, there is always the chance that one of them will slot home a goal, which is why you need every opportunity of your own to be fully exploited in the final third.

To lose 2-0 is not the end of the world. If you look at the Premier League teams with newish managers this weekend, none of them lost. The record of fresh appointments read three wins and one draw.

Eddie Howe oversaw a 3-3 draw for Newcastle against Brentford. Smith is now in charge at Norwich, they beat Southampton 2-1. Claudio Rainieri and Watford won 4-1 at home to Manchester United, causing another manager in Ole Gunnar Solksjaer to lose his job.

Gerrard got his new club three points from Aston Villa 2-0 Brighton. And Antonio Conte and Spurs beat Leeds 2-1.

They call this the new manager bounce effect. Villa, Newcastle, Watford, and Norwich might be benefiting from it now, but it does not last for too long as players lose their eagerness to impress the new manager beyond those initial few weeks.

Another game to keep an eye on at the weekend was Liverpool v Arsenal, where the Gunners lost 4-0 at Anfield. Only three weeks earlier, we had gone to Liverpool and drawn 2-2, suggesting we are not in a bad place.

Brighton's squad is young and will improve through learning from this seven-game winless run, which will end very soon.

The efforts at Villa Park of Leandro Trossard, Tariq Lamptey and Jakub Moder were to be applauded. Jason Steele also made some important saves on his Premier League debut.

Listening at home via BBC Radio Sussex, it sounded like a very loud Villa crowd to start with. I was really pleased to hear our travelling support making a lot of noise as the game wore on to drown out the home fans.

The familiar chants of Albion fans are always a comfort as I really miss seeing the game. Johnny Cantor and Warren Aspinall do a good job, but it is still frustrating when somebody tells you it is a free kick and you do not know which team has it.

Still, there will be less need to listen on the radio with such a packed fixture list coming up. This Saturday, we have the joys of watching Leeds United at the Amex as Marcelo Bielsa tried to coach his team to their third league win of the season.

Graham Potter has been putting in the hours, watching Bielsa and Leeds live. Those with eagle eyes tuned into that Spurs v Leeds game on Sunday may have seen the Sky cameras zoom in on Potter and Billy Reid watching from the stands.

It was not just Leeds who they were there to make some notes on. Brighton also face Spurs at the Amex on Sunday December 12th, so this was a timely day out for both Potter and Reid, who are certainly doing everything they can to try and give the squad every bit of help and advice possible.

I wonder what they made of Antonio Conte getting very animated with the crowd at the Tottenham Hotspur Stadium. He was being very, very Italian and it certainly got the Spurs fans going.

We will need to be in similar voice, making lots of noise against Leeds this Saturday. Up the Albion.

Leeds a lesson in the danger of leaving late to get to the Amex
November 27th 2021

Brighton 0 Leeds 0

When they say leave plenty of time to get to the Amex, they really do mean it. Due to my better half being committed until 3pm on the day that Leeds United visited, we could not set off for the stadium until 3.30pm, leaving just two hours to get there in time for kick off. We caught the 16.01 train from Haywards Heath which was full of people wearing red and white scarves and bobble hats. I thought this strange as Leeds do not wear red and white, so who were these people?

Realisation dawned that they were Arsenal fans returning to their Sussex homes after their lunchtime game against Newcastle United.

The Gunners had won 2-0 so they were in good voice. With the train also containing Seagulls supporters and some Leeds fan, it was a real mixed audience as we sped towards Brighton.

On arrival at Brighton Station with now only one hour until kick off, the mass exodus gave away to massive queues to board trains to Falmer.

The Leeds supporters were singing loud and proud, making their presence felt – even if they were somewhat confused to see so many Arsenal fans in Brighton.

Whilst Leeds went through their repertoire of songs, I took stock of the queue and alarm bells began ringing. At the rate it was currently moving, we would miss the start of the game.

This was unheard of and so the option of a taxi was discussed. On arrival at the taxi rank, there were no cars to be found. Five minutes passed with still zero taxis and so it was back to the queue and hoping that we made it onto a train.

We just made it through the gates and onto the platform, where we then waited for the station staff to allow the crowd to approach the train.

The organisation at this point was terrible. Too many people had been allowed onto the platform and the metal barriers designed to send the huge queues on a tight and snaking funnel could not cope.

Inevitably, the sheer weight of people made the barriers go over and injuries looked imminent. Who teaches these people to steward a crowd? They obviously do no remember the Hillsborough Disaster.

For me at least, it was not too different from my commuting days packed onto London Underground trains like sardines. At Brighton Station though, there were women and young supporters in danger.

The management of the queue needs reviewing or else I fear someone will get crushed and seriously injured in the not-too-distant future.

Once out of the nightmare queue and onto a train, we arrived at Falmer within minutes. A quick trek up to the stadium and we were seated just in time for the teams to emerge. It was all too close to comfort for me, leaving no time to buy sweets or a programme.

There were fireworks to celebrate LGBTQ+ via the Rainbow Laces campaign, marked throughout the Premier League over the weekend.

As far as I am aware, nobody went as far as the Albion's pyrotechnics but then again, we always stand out when it comes to these sorts of things.

Brighton found themselves kicking towards the North Stand in the first half. We were all over Leeds, a far cry from Spurs last Sunday who were run ragged by Leeds and lucky not to be a couple of goals down before half time.

The Albion had clearly devised a game plan to ensure Leeds would not be so effective at the Amex, hardly a surprise seeing as Graham Potter and Billy Reid were both in the crowd at the Tottenham Hotspur Stadium a week ago.

Nobody could fault the effort of the players, who worked their socks off to stay on the front foot and keep Leeds at bay.

It was just unfortunate that the opportunities we had failed to go in. That is football, some days are like that. Just look at Chelsea against Manchester United on Sunday afternoon who, for all their efforts, had still not managed to score by half time.

Leandro Trossard kept hitting the woodwork, Jakub Moder just missed a couple of opportunities, and so on and so on. On another day, those types of chances will go in. It just wasn't to be.

Trossard was brilliant in weaving around defenders. Solly March looked lively when he came on and was unlucky not to score. Tariq Lamptey played a blinder in getting his marker booked so early and then substituted at half time.

We also owe a debt of gratitude to Robert Sanchez who had to make three great saves to ensure that it finished 0-0. Had we lost, it would have been a travesty.

With all the hard graft and effort that the team put in, there was absolutely no excuse for the booing at the end of the match.

The spectators that did so are just that – spectators – and not true Albion supporters. Like those who seem to come to the Amex just to drink rather than support the team.

I am always amazed by their numbers – although not as amazed as I am that the ladies toilet in the East Upper has been blocked for over a month now. Get it sorted prior to the Spurs game, please Albion.

Before then, the Albion are off to the London Stadium on Wednesday evening for a tough match against West Ham. The Hammers are playing really well at the moment and sit fourth in the table, but as we know Brighton tend to do better against stronger teams.

Hopefully, facing such opponents will take our guys onto the sort of level we saw in the 2-2 draw at Liverpool.

Following our night in the East End, it is down to Southampton on Saturday to face Ralph Hasenhüttl's side who lost 4-0 to Liverpool on Saturday afternoon.

It is all to play for this week. If we think positive and hope that lady luck comes our way, then there is enough skill in this young squad to continue their push for a top 10 place by the end of the season.

More chanting and less booing would help. Ignore those who only come to the Amex to spectate – it is the real Albion fans that count.

Has Amazon Prime had a better sight than Graham Potter jumping for joy?
November 30th 2021

West Ham 1 Brighton 1

Wednesday night's trip to West Ham United kicked off a busy December period for Brighton of seven games crammed into 29 days.

Whether you watched from the London Stadium, via Amazon Prime for the first time this season, or listened along with Johnny Cantor and Warren Aspinall on BBC Radio Sussex, a meeting with the Hammers was always going to be a tough game.

It is one of those quirks of football that, despite West Ham being a quality football outfit, they had not beaten the Albion in eight previous Premier League meetings.

Make that nine now thanks to Neal Maupay and his amazing scissor kick in the final minute as it finished West Ham 1-1 Brighton.

I opted to watch this one alone, giving up my usual place on the lounge settee and instead shutting the bungalow doors to the kitchen diner area where the action was beamed live onto our 55-inch TV via Amazon.

This proved a good decision when the 89th minute rolled around as I am not sure if the already-worn springs on the settee could take the sort of reaction that Maupay's goal might have subjected them to.

The first thing to say is that the picture quality of Amazon was absolutely superb. They had all six Wednesday night games available to watch, followed by both Thursday evening matches. A real treat if you like live football.

West Ham put on a colourful start before kick-off with fireworks and a light show to support the Rainbow Laces campaign. Although impressive, it was not as good as the Rainbow Laces display, we saw at the Amex against Leeds United at the weekend.

Kick off at the London Stadium was at 7:30pm. By 7:31pm, Maupay had missed the first opportunity of the evening, which I am sure gave everyone a feeling of deja vu following the frustrations of the Leeds match.

It came a no surprise that moments after Maupay squandered that early chance, West Ham banged on Robert Sanchez's goal to win an early corner.

Danger! Alarm bells immediately rang for me, as I am sure they did for other Brighton fans and even the team themselves. Overcame a cracking corner taken by Pablo Fornals, whose in-swinger glanced off Tomáš Souček's head to put the Hammers 1-0 up after only five minutes.

Brighton now had it all to do and by heck they put in a real shift which took a toll on several bodies. Albion players started dropping like flies and Graham Potter had to use his substitutes far sooner than he would have anticipated.

Jeremy Sarmiento went down first with what looked like a hamstring injury in the 12th minute. It was a real shame for him and for us Brighton supporters because this was the debut of a young talent, we are all very excited about.

I am sure he has a great deal to offer and will grasp the chance to show everyone exactly what he can do and bring to the team – it is just a shame that we now have to wait a few months to see it.

Next to fall was one of our solid back three, Adam Webster. He initially went down holding his calf and having recently returned from injury, it was a real concern.

After having physios on the pitch for treatment he initially battled on, but alas had to concede to the injury a few minutes later.

Potter replaced Webster with Shane Duffy, which did at least give Brighton a stronger aerial presence to try and deal with any further West Ham set pieces.

The half time whistle went after significant time added on to cover the injuries. With the way the opening 45 minutes had gone, I felt sure that West Ham would score again before the game was out.

They did manage to put the ball in the back of the net, but it was thankfully disallowed. VAR took a very long look at what had happened before deciding to rule in the Albion's favour.

Sanchez still had to make some excellent acrobatic saves from numerous West Ham attempts on goal. Those stops set the scene for Maupay to come through in the dying moments with that most brilliant goal to put the Albion back level.

To see Graham Potter and Billy Reid jumping for joy in the technical area was a wonderful sight. The seats in the away dugout and the terraces at the London Stadium may have taken a bashing, but at least my settee springs did not.

Even when injury ravaged, this Brighton team will just not lose
December 4th 2021

Southampton 1 Brighton 1

It was a windy but dry afternoon to start with on Saturday at St Mary's according to our BBC Radio Sussex commentary team Johnny Cantor and Warren Aspinall. Soon though, the weather in Southampton was the least of anyone's concerns.

For when the Brighton starting XI was announced, it showed that the Albion's injury problems were worsening. Captain Lewis Dunk was missing due to a knee injury, and it was confirmed after the game that he will be out until at least the start of 2022.

By the time the final whistle blew, Leandro Trossard had left on a stretcher and Joel Veltman departed after a blow to the face.

Veltman is also one booking away from a suspension. Shane Duffy picked up his fifth yellow at Southampton meaning he misses the next game, either against Spurs depending on their Covid outbreak or Wolves on Wednesday night.

With Adam Webster also ruled out, oh my God, we have no back three! Haydon Roberts may find himself being used. He has looked ready for a Premier League debut.

There are other players who are capable stepping up, showing the strength Graham Potter has built in his squad. It will be needed when you also remember the absence of Adam Lallana and Danny Welbeck.

Potter made five changes from West Ham 1-1 Brighton. That point at the London Stadium looks even better a week on than it did at the time, having seen the mighty Chelsea beaten 3-2 by the Hammers on Saturday.

I think the Albion deserve to be commended for playing so well and fighting right to the end against opponents who proved themselves good enough to beat the European Champions.

Similar fight and belief was on display at Southampton. The commentators reported good support at St Mary's, where apparently there were some 3,000 travelling Albion fans.

A calm first few minutes gave way to a busy period for Robert Sanchez. He made two great saves in the first six minutes. Enoch Mwepu, unfortunately, had a chance that was not to his liking, but it was still early days.

Listening to the radio creates a mental picture in your mind of what is going on. The picture I was given by our commentators after that action packed start, was that a couple of misplaced passes from Sanchez had given Southampton several quick breaks back towards our own goal.

This was worrying and eventually, the inevitable happened. Deep sigh, Southampton went 1-0 ahead. The goal was reported as coming from scrappy play from Brighton, another poor kick from Sanchez being sent back and Armando Broja took advantage to score with 29 minutes played.

Duffy picked up the booking we really needed him to avoid in the 44th minute. It sounded like Duffy was being pulled out of position on many occasions to cover for his teammates who were struggling and eventually, this led to him being dealt a yellow card.

It was only a matter of time I suppose; Duffy is one of those players who puts in 120 percent all the time for the team and that comes with risks.

Only one added minute was needed, and I rushed to bung the kettle on the moment the half time whistle sounded. Whilst it boiled, I breathed a sigh of relief that we were only one goal behind at the break.

Another poor clearance from Sanchez kicked off the second half. The commentators were concerned that little seemed to have changed for Brighton and began thinking out loud that Potter needed to do something to influence the game.

The manager's answer was to bring on Aaron Connolly for Pascal Gross. Tariq Lamptey was substituted a short while later for Solly March as Potter looked to alter the dynamics which, up to this point, had been total control of midfield by Southampton.

A chance came and went for Maupay before Veltman headed straight down the tunnel to be replaced by Jakub Moder. Moder went close but it was not to be as Brighton still struggled to play their possession football.

Even though their usual style was missing, the Albion continued to give their all, believing they could get back into it just as they had done at West Ham.

The commentators mentioned that Southampton began timewasting with quite a while still left to play. Trossard's injury and treatment meant that significant time would have to be added on at the end, even before the home team's antics.

It looked like a nasty wrist injury for Trossard, and he was carried off with a brace on his right arm. Warren was not impressed with the reaction of the medical team, saying: "The St Johns Ambulance team were so slow, that he could walk backwards faster than that!"

The commentary also revealed that it was Trossard's birthday. Not a very pleasant present for him to be wheeled away on a stretcher. Let us hope it is not as serious as it first looked.

Brighton were now finishing the game with 10 men, just as they had at West Ham. The fourth official announced a further 10 minutes of injury time to be played, giving the Albion time on their side to keep plugging away.

March and Moder were both working hard to break Southampton down. Then the moment arrived. A free kick taken by Moder just outside Southampton's penalty area on the left side rebounded off the wall.

Moder chipped the ball at quite some pace past the wall at the second attempt. Neal Maupay was right there, clearly onside when you watch the clip back on the Albion website, and he turned to hit the ball into the corner of the Southampton goal.

With literally minutes left, Brighton had rescued a point with 10 men again. It was breath taking. I mentioned déjà vu last week and yes, once again, our musketeer named Neal – not Athos, Porthos or Aramis – but Neal scored to save the day.

This Brighton team will just not lose. They give it their all. They always do and I am sure always will. It was so lovely to hear and later see the highlights.

The past two matches have made me so proud of our team. Now it is time for the squad to step up and drop into those vacant slots to give the injured parties time to recover.

They can do it, as their fight against West Ham and Southampton has shown. Brighton are the definition of it never being over until the fat lady sings.

Reasons to moan post-Wolves – but the result wasn't one of them
December 11th 2021

Brighton 0   Wolves 1

There were a few reasons to moan and groan when Wolves came to the Amex, but the final score was not one of them. You just have to look at what happened to Leeds who were beaten 7-0 by Manchester City to see a truly bad result.

Perhaps when the Seagulls concede seven unanswered goals, then we can start to air our concerns about the football. We only lost 1-0 to Wolves, and their fans could not have been impressed by their performance as they did not play too well either.

What Wolves did do is defend superbly even as both sides missed opportunities. Marçal in particular had an excellent game, shutting down the threat that is Tariq Lamptey down the right.

That impressive team defensive display stretched into Wolves' next game on Sunday when they drew 0-0 with Chelsea, highlighting what a good side they are.

One thing that definitely deserved to be moaned about was the number of Albion fans still refusing to mask up, both on the train and at the Amex.

What is wrong with these people? Perhaps they need to spend some time in the Covid wards at the Sussex County Hospital. Then they may be less likely to ignore the medical advice on offer.

On arriving at the Amex amongst the maskless, things looked much quieter than normal. Supporters appeared to be staying away as a result of the media and warnings relating to how easily the omicron variant can spread.

For a December evening, it was surprisingly mild weather-wise. That was in contrast to the Wolves supporters swelling the South Stand, who did their best to create an atmosphere that was anything but mild by being in good voice.

It felt like the whole of Wolverhampton had made the trip and they made the North Stand vocalists sound like a children's choir. Seagulls supporters seem to be lacking in enthusiasm to cheer on the team at home recently and I cannot work out why that should be.

With so many players absent through injury and suspension, Dan Burn captained the side. At the start of the game, I looked across to the players' viewing area which was busier than the North Stand with all those unable to play jostling for a seat.

Brighton had first half chances, but they mainly slipped away. The Albion seemed to have trouble gelling with their passing game being less accurate than normal.

Still, it looked like we would make it to the break at 0-0 until the first half entered time added on. A Wolves corner which appeared to be badly taken was not cleared and the ball was chipped back into Romain Saiss.

He got a foot to it and suddenly, Brighton were 1-0 down. Disappointed was not the word. There was an instant chance to reply but Enock Mwepu was unlucky when a shot went just over the bar.

Robert Sanchez performed some great saves yet again as the second half began, Wolves' Daniel Podence putting our goalkeeper to the test on more than one occasion.

Towards the end of the game, it got more exciting for the Albion as we piled on the pressure. The game stretched to 100 minutes thanks to problems with referee Mr Tony Harrington's communication equipment.

It was Mr Harrington's Premier League debut, and he is unlikely to forget it. Numerous times the game had to be stopped and, in the end, it became quite painful.

Brighton fans of course aired their views relating to Mr Harrington's unfortunate situation, which finally forced him to leave the pitch to try and get it sorted once and for all.

As the game headed toward its 10th minute of stoppage time, Brighton won a series of corners in front of the North Stand. These drew Sanchez up, but they only allowed Wolves to again show how strong they are defensively as the Albion were unable to force an equaliser.

There was no sign of giving up from the Albion, but it just wasn't to be this week – unlike the West Ham and Southampton games when Brighton brought things back from the edge late on.

So many people after the game started running the team down and there is no need for that sort of criticism for the side that was named against Wolves. Bearing in mind it was a backup team because of the numbers missing, they did well.

The Albion continued their policy of announcing crowd attendance figures which reflect tickets sold, not the number of people actually in the ground – even when on this occasion the difference was laughable.

God knows what would happen in an emergency. Do the club have any idea how many fans are in the actual stadium? Those who were there need some choir practice if we are to up the noise for the next home game, be that Brentford on Boxing Day or another date in the future if Covid continues to disrupt the Premier League.

The mask situation leaving the Amex was similar to that on arrival – many stupid people not bothering and putting all at risk. To make matters worse, the vocal Wolves fans decided to urinate off the upper levels of the gantry above Falmer Station.

It is not against the law to urinate in public, however local by-laws may have regulations. I just felt sorry for people below who may of thought it had started to rain. I am afraid stewards are not up to the task and it is not fair they should have to deal with such situations.

The lack of recent football is at least giving the squad time to recover and get fit for the games ahead. Hopefully, Graham Potter can find a way to return us to our form from earlier in the season.

I for one am looking forward to the next five months of the season and hope to see many more points added to our tally. Merry Christmas everyone and a happy and healthy 2022. Up the Albion!

All aboard! Boxing Day on the bus made worthwhile as Albion sting Bees
December 26th 2021

Brighton 2 Brentford 0

Belated season's greetings everyone… and what a late Christmas present we had on Boxing Day evening at the Amex as the Albion ended that winless run with a 2-0 success over Brentford.

My planning to get to the stadium and back from North Sussex had begun in mid-October when it became apparent there would be no public transport.

The best bet looked to be booking early to avoid disappointment with our trusted travel firm Seagull Travel. As those meerkats say, "simples".

I went onto the booking site and secured two return tickets from Seaford Station, driving and parking nearby and then boarding the bus to the Amex.

Boy, was it worth it? The Seagull Travel team are real professionals and made the whole experience really easy. It must have taken a military-style operation to organise as I have never seen so many buses and coaches in my life all in the one place.

We worked out if the visitors' South Stand was full with its normal 3000 visiting fans, Brentford would have needed around 60 hire coaches themselves for their supporters. That gives you an idea of how many buses were required to get Albion fans to and from the Amex from all over Sussex.

The Brentford end however was only half full. The Brighton sections were around the same. We all know why. A Boxing Day 8pm kick combined with the dreaded Covid-19 problem, something we avoided both before and after the game with a negative test returned on Monday. Funnily enough, no official attendance was announced at the game.

Two bits of punditry caught my eye in the lead up to the game, both from Sky Sports. It was reported that Brighton had led for only 42 minutes through the last 11 games. What does that even mean as a statistic?

Paul Merson also said that we did not have any natural goal scorers. Maybe he should eat his words after Neal Maupay and Leandro Trossard scored two excellent goals? All I can say to pundits like this is watch this space as you write the Albion off at your peril.

There is always something extra exciting about Boxing Day football. It takes me back to my childhood days watching at the Goldstone Ground, when seeing the Albion over Christmas was a real treat and something to look forward to.

When Trossard opened the scoring, my wife said to me: "Calm down and sit down before you have a heart attack". I couldn't help myself… when the Albion score goals, all is well in the world.

My late dad – who was a Hove Grammar School Boy in the 1930s and was far cleverer than me by the way – would have been so proud of the Albion these days, competing in the top division with the best teams in the land.

He played football until he was 45 years of age for Hove Grammar School Old Boys most weeks. Their home pitch was in Hove Park, a stone's throw from the Goldstone. I still remember the roars that came from the ground, even today.

Strangely, the noise that was made throughout Brighton 2-0 Brentford was louder than when the Amex has over 30,000 spectators in it. You could see the difference it made to the players who obviously need lots of vocal support.

I feel sometimes that we as fans need to make more noise, like the travelling Everton and Wolves fans did when they visited the south coast this season.

Brighton were able to welcome back several players returning from injury. The team appeared to be really up for it, putting in 120 percent and chasing down every ball.

The Albion also had the rub of the green as they say in golf. Moments of luck seem to have avoided us in recent months but on this occasion, the ball was kind to us.

Not many men in blue and white slipped over either, compared to the 1-0 defeat to Wolves when players seemed to hit the ground regularly. Perhaps the ground staff have realised that the pitch need not be overwatered?

Both Maupay and Trossard pressed the Brentford goalkeeper hard early on, as if they smelt blood and were desperate to force an error. This proved sensible as Alvaro Fernandez did look a little shaky. Unfortunately, nothing ended up coming of it.

Early attacking play from the Seagulls laid down a pattern of what was to come during the game. Brentford could have posed a real threat through Ivan Toney and Bryan Mbeumo but Adam Webster returning in a back four along with Dan Burn and Tariq Lamptey did extremely well to control the Bees' strikers.

Burn made a big start to the game, preventing Mbeumo getting a shot away in the first two minutes and then clearing from behind Robert Sanchez when a long ball forward allowed Mbeumo to chip over the Albion goalkeeper. It would have been given as offside; however, Burn was not to know that at the time.

Up the other end and Burn hit the crossbar with a header from a beautifully taken Alexis Mac Allister corner. A great ball from Sanchez out to Marc Cucurella sent him off to cross smartly for Enock Mwepu.

Mwepu's shot flew past the post from seven yards out. A good chance missed but that he gets into those positions means that more opportunities will continue to come for Mwepu over the second half of the season.

Possession was around 50-50 as the game reached the 30-minute mark, indicating how even it had been. The deadlock was then broken when an exquisite forward pass from Mwepu found the perfectly timed run of Trossard from an onside position.

Fernandez committed to coming to the edge of his penalty area and Trossard connected to the ball dropping out of the sky with his left foot, lifting it over the head of the Brentford goalkeeper to make it 1-0.

It was a brilliant goal followed by the excitement of fans going mad. No need to worry about jumping into anyone during the celebrations and knocking fellow fans over – we had nobody near us at all.

What we needed in the remaining 11 minutes of the first half was a second goal. As luck would have it, that is just what we got by the way of Maupay hitting a perfect shot into the top right corner of the Brentford net. Fernandez had no chance and credit should also go to Jakub Moder for a great assist.

Brighton might have added a third in the early stages of four minutes of stoppage time. A free kick was awarded just outside the D of the Brentford penalty area. Trossard lined up to take it just a little off to the left, but he put it straight down the throat of Fernandez.

The second half brought the return of Danny Welbeck in place of the injured Trossard and some amazing saves from Sanchez. Despite Thomas Frank giving his team a hard talking to during the break, I felt that Brighton would go onto add to the score in the second half.

That was not to be despite the Albion continuing to push and not falling back on their laurels. Instead, it was Sanchez who made an astounding save in the 59th minute, managing to get a leg to a deflected shot by Shandon Baptiste.

Less than a minute later and Sanchez's amazing agility kept the ball out of the Albion net following a header from Ethan Pinnock. It was another brilliant stop that ended up preserving a clean sheet but not without a little pain, Sanchez colliding his shoulder with the post.

Cucurella was next to deny Brentford, heading off the line from Pinnock as Brentford persisted in trying to prevent Brighton earning a shutout.

The Albion though got there, leaving fans as pleased as chairman Tony Bloom who was watching on from the director's box.

The only task remaining afterwards was to find the bus home. With coaches everywhere – busier than Southdown Pool Valley ever used to be – that proved to be the hardest part of a brilliant Boxing Day.

Prime coverage, poor punditry, and Albion camaraderie on show at Chelsea
January 1st 2022

Chelsea 1 Brighton 1

For Wednesday night's trip to Chelsea, Amazon Prime provided my viewing platform and once again the late drama supplied by Danny Welbeck and Brighton meant that my poor settee springs were in for a tough time – a recurring theme so far this season.

Not that I should complain. We are lucky to get to see more game these days than in years gone by on TV through various media means available to us, even if some of these do not come cheaply.

For those who cannot afford the increasing cost of the subscriptions needed, BBC Radio Sussex provide a fantastic service for free to those of us living in the county.

Johnny Cantor and Warren Aspinall on commentary are full of lots of useful information, although in this case it was debatable whether we wanted to hear that the last time Brighton found the back of the net at Stamford Bridge was a 1923 FA Cup tie against Corinthian, or that the Albion had never scored a goal away against Chelsea. Perhaps we could hold them to a 0-0 draw again…

Even before hearing that statistic, I think most Brighton fans probably would have thought before the match that the Albion may struggle against the European Champions – especially with the depth of squad that Thomas Tuchel has at his disposal at Chelsea.

Having played just three days ago when beating Brentford 2-0, Graham Potter made three changes from the Boxing Day win. Those changes brought back Yves Bissouma, Joel Veltman and Solly March.

Straight from kick off, you could see it was going to be a fast-moving encounter. Our back four comprising of Tariq Lamptey, Veltman, Dan Burn and Marc Cucurella gave it everything. They chased every ball and put in several robust but fair challenges.

That was in stark contrast to Antonio Rudiger, who was lucky not to be sent off with a dangerous challenge on our Tariq which gained Rudiger a yellow card. Lamptey would have left him standing if he had passed him and Rudiger knew it, so he fouled him.

I was astounded that the Prime pitch side guest Eni Aluko said on camera at half time that it was a fair tackle on Lamptey. Dream on! It was nothing less than a second-rate chop!

Where did she play her football again? Oh yes, Chelsea Women. Brighton Women should watch out when they face the Blues if that is what they teach as fair at the Chelsea Academy.

It was in the 27th minute that Romelo Lukaku headed home Chelsea's goal. At that point, I thought here we go. We had done well up to that point but surely the quality of the Blues would now show through.

Instead, hey, this just fired the Albion up. Great chances came our way as the lads settled into the game with Adam Lallana, Alexis Mac Allister, Jakub Moder and Neal Maupay all having opportunities.

Veltman had to make a couple of good defensive plays. He did so well to prevent Callum Hudson-Odoi from scoring for Chelsea in the second half when clearing off the line. Also standing out was his ability in the air; he was a real stalwart in this game.

Welbeck came on as a sub for Mac Allister late on and that eventually led to another 90 plus grandstand finish. An exquisite delivery from Cucurella was straight onto Welbeck and his header down into the left-hand corner easily had the beating of Chelsea goalkeeper Edouard Mendy with less than two minutes of time added on to play.

I was elated at such a great goal at a decisive time, as I am sure everyone reading this was. This really cannot go on like this however, as the settee springs took another bashing.

The result certainly gave Tuchel the real grumps and that made it feel even more like a win than it already did through the lateness of the equaliser. That determination to not sit back and continue to battle until the very last whistle really shows through.

I compared our game with Manchester United against Burnley 24 hours later, where Burnley were turned over whilst putting in nowhere near the effort that our lads did at Chelsea.

Following the Brentford and Chelsea matches, it has become even clearer to those of us who have followed the Albion's weekly activities very closely that they really seem to be gelling together so well as a squad.

They appear to be playing for each other and if you watch, the camaraderie of the team and the squad looks brilliant. Long may it continue. This type of togetherness, playing as a team and not squabbling with each other will lead to inevitable success.

That is not to say of course that we are not already enjoying success, because we are. Brighton sit 10th in the Premier League ahead of a trip to Everton which kicks off 2022.

We have now played 18 games and have 24 points with two games in hand on some of our competitors. If the Albion can continue to build on their recent successes over the holiday period, then the next 12 months could be even more fantastic than the previous.

Following Everton, Brighton visit West Bromwich Albion in the FA Cup. That is followed by an 8pm Friday night kick off against rivals Crystal Palace. Nobody needs reminding of the importance of that.

So, there is lots to play for over the next few weeks. The squad appear to be mentally in a good place – and if Leandro Trossard can return to join the fun at Goodison, who knows what might happen? Up Albion!

One week, seven points: An amazing festive effort from the Albion
January 1st 2022

Everton 2 Brighton 3

What a display we have been treated to by the Albion over the Christmas and New Year week. Three tough games in the space of seven days and we pick up seven points from a possible nine.

Other managers complain about fixture congestion and Brighton just get on with it. An amazing effort by the squad, whose success has been well deserved. All I can now say is a very big thank you to the players for a really entertaining holiday period of football.

Brighton saved the best of the three games until last. Before Sunday, the Albion had never won an away game at Goodison Park and so a little bit of history was written in Everton 2-3 Brighton as the Seagulls broke that spell.

Those of us based in Sussex and not able to travel to Everton had the pleasure of tuning into Johnny Cantor and Warren Aspinall on BBC Radio Sussex.

Licensing laws prevent the coverage being broadcast outside of the local area, but Albion fans located in other parts of the world could still listen via the Brighton website.

Be warned though, the delay is such that you will often be notified about a goal before you hear about it as the audio through the internet is one to two minutes behind real time. I fell foul of that when on holiday earlier in the season!

The Albion support certainly sounded noisy over the radio. Although I have never been to Goodison Park myself, I know it to be an old-style ground which these days can hold 39,414 when full.

That Brighton fans could be heard over the Everton support was impressive as the home fans backed their team loudly, especially in the second half when they got on top.

You can only imagine the noise present when Goodison had its record attendance, 78,299 according to the archives for an Everton vs Liverpool game on September 18th, 1948. Luckily, it was not that full on Sunday.

Graham Potter made three changes to the side from the game at Chelsea on Wednesday night. Most of us were still on an amazing high from that 1-1 draw at Stamford Bridge.

I don't know about you guys, but I felt so proud of the squad recently for all the super effort and togetherness they have shown in every game.

The changes were Leonardo Trossard, Enoch Mwepu and Adam Webster all returning to the side to start the game.

Everton had back in their line up striker Dominic Calvert-Lewin, who had been out with injury since his visit to the Amex back in late August 2021. The Toffees won 2-0 that day.

Brighton started their first game of 2022 very well. In fact, amazingly well. With three minutes, Alexis Mac Allister scored the first goal of the afternoon for the Seagulls.

It did require a VAR check, leaving all our hearts in our mouths. Mac Allister though had timed his run to the perfection to finish off a great move.

The cross from Joel Veltman was excellent and followed by a great header down by Neal Maupay to the feet of Mac Alister.

Maupay showed great thinking to get the ball to Mac Allister. The fantastic start ensured that the old settee springs began another journey through hell much earlier than normal.

Then of course you start, come on lads, one is not enough. The players seemed to share that opinion and in the 21st minute, Dan Burn made it 2-0 with his first goal of the season. It was exactly what we needed, players other than the forwards getting a chance to have a go and taking it.

The highlights showed poor Everton marking left Burn free at the far post from the corner – but he still had to put the ball into the back of the net. The build-up to the goal deserved praise too, Mwepu superbly flicking on an excellent deliver from Mac Allister.

Yves Bissouma played his part in winning the corner. He ploughed up field, weaving and dodging Everton defenders to get a shot away which was just deflected over the bar. Once again, it was great play from Bissouma.

There was plenty more drama to come. Anthony Gordon for Everton definitely got nudged in the area by Mwepu and went down.

Play continued for a short while until the ball went out. It was then that referee John Brooks was asked by VAR to view the incident on the touchline screen.

Mr Brooks did not take long to award Everton a penalty with Calvert-Lewin stepping up to take it. He went for the top corner, but the ball instead flew over the bar.

It was a bad miss from Calvert-Lewin, whose last goal ironically had been a penalty against Brighton at the Amex. The relief at him failing to score this time meant another bashing for those settee springs.

Even when the game entered three minutes of first half injury time, the action was not done. Adam Lallana had a shot just pushed past the post by Jordan Pickford. It was all still happening.

Despite Brighton having a clear two goal lead as the half time whistle blew, we knew that Everton would improve. Rafa Benitez would be lighting up the home dressing room with perhaps more than just a little chat to his players.

It took eight minutes of the second half for Everton to finally score. It was rather unlucky for the Albion as the shot was deflected off Lallana and past Robert Sanchez to make it 2-1.

I thought to myself, can we hold onto this lead, or will we draw 2-2? I expect that is what most of us were wondering.

Then came an amazing goal from Mac Allister that many pundits have likened to something from Lionel Messi. You know it is a good volley when it gives England number one Pickford no chance.

Trossard had chipped a ball back into the D and a great little flick from Mwepu teed up Mac Allister for his rocket. Everton 1-3 Brighton and the upper hand was back with the Seagulls.

Just five minutes later however, Gordon scored his second of the game for Everton. Oh my god I thought, they are going to come at us in the final 15 minutes. And they did.

The Goodison crowd was re-aroused and Johnny and Warren on the radio sounded a little panicked as the Albion goal was peppered by Everton.

Brighton were seemingly struggling but they continued to fight on. Everton were desperate to scrape the draw but no, the Albion held on for a famous 3-2 victory to complete an amazing festive week.

Now roll-on West Bromwich Albion in the FA Cup.

Slow start, powerful finish, an FA Cup win, and chores down in the garage
January 11th 2022

West Brom 1 Brighton 2

I really enjoy listening to Johnny Cantor and Warren Aspinall with their commentary on BBC Radio Sussex. Obviously, I miss seeing the action at away games I cannot attend but as far as second options go, you would be hard pressed to find better coverage than we Brighton fans are treated to on the radio.

Not much must have happened in the first half at the Hawthorns as not even Johnny and Warren could make it sound interesting.

The only nugget of information standing out from the radio commentary was that ex-Seagulls goalkeeper David Button was in goal for the Baggies.

The slow start can probably be attributed to both teams trying to find their level with many new faces. Brighton made seven changes including goalkeeper Kjell Scherpen, who had to neatly take a West Brom opportunity in the first couple of minutes of his debut. That was followed up by a Baggies effort over the Albion bar.

Scherpen did not have an awful lot more to worry about. It looks and sounds as if he is quite a unique goalkeeper; I wonder if he might benefit from a loan spell to help him get minutes under his belt?

It sounded as though West Brom had plenty of pace going through the middle. Johnny and Warren indicated that sloppy play was costing Brighton early on.

For the first time in a long time, I began to worry about our chances in a game as it did not appear to be happening for the Seagulls.

Danny Welbeck then had the first Brighton chance in the 19th minute when he went one-on-one with Button. Button had a point to prove against his former team, that made it hard for Welbeck and sadly the goal did not materialise.

Half time arrived with the score at 0-0. With there being nothing for the radio to ponder over or analyse, I found myself going out to the garage to do a quick chore, hoping that Graham Potter could introduced some words of wisdom to give the team a helping hand in the second half.

What I had hoped for did not initially happen. In fact, it was the reverse. Two minutes into the second half and Callum Robinson of the Baggies slotted a cross past Scherpen to put West Brom ahead.

Referee Robert Jones had appeared to be extremely lenient in the first half. Fans of both clubs in the 8,000 crowd – including a sizable number of the famous Seagulls away support – certainly let him know what they thought each time he made (or failed to make) a decision.

Mr Jones' leniency disappeared around the hour mark. Cédric Kipré received a yellow card for a nasty hit on Neal Maupay in the centre circle.

Then in a flash, Kipré fouled Leandro Trossard down the right side to earn a second booking from Mr Jones. The Baggies were down to 10 men and things might just be looking up for the Seagulls, I thought.

Perhaps I had been overly negative before? When you cannot see what is happening, it is quite frustrating as your brain sometimes plays tricks on you and everything seems a lot worse than it is.

The free kick from Trossard being fouled by Kipré was delivered and well placed for skipper-for-the-day Shane Duffy to put the ball over the bar, missing a real chance to draw the Seagulls level.

Now we had some excitement. We know from this season that Brighton never give up. Potter made some final changes, Joel Veltman giving way to young striker Evan Ferguson and Steve Alzate coming off for Jakub Moder.

It was Moder who scored a great goal to bring the Seagulls level at 1-1. He finished with his left foot as he ran right to left across the goal, ably assisted by Ferguson.

Ferguson was next to have an attempt. The ball went just over the crossbar and landed on the roof of the net. What an impact the 17-year-old had during his time on the pitch.

Alexis Mac Allister had his turn next to be denied by Button, who pushed a low shot down to the left away. The tempo was starting to build as the Seagulls looked to swoop in for a second goal so that we might all avoid another 30 minutes with no replays in the competition this year.

The goal never came, and so extra time was needed to decide the tie. As we have seen so many times this season, Maupay had waited for his moment and eight minutes into the additional 30, he made it West Brom 1-2 Brighton.

That had me out of my seat, settee springs getting their familiar bashing and tea spilt everywhere. It is a good job I am not a commentator; screaming "OH MY GOD" over and over would not give much clue to what is happening to those listening at home. I cannot help but get excited; one day I am sure I will give myself a heart attack.

It was all a far cry from the first half which had driven me into the garage. There was nearly more joy when Moder raced down the left to cross for Ferguson who slotted the ball confidently past Button.

Disappointingly, Ferguson had been offside. That goal may have been chalked off, but it will surely not be long before the young man scores for Brighton.

Trossard went close to making it 3-1 but in the end, two goals were enough for the Albion. Ball 10 came out the fourth round draw the following day for a trip to the Tottenham Hotspur Stadium to face Spurs. Is it too soon to dream of Wembley?

Before that, we have three tough games coming up in the next 10 days. This Friday is Crystal Palace at the Amex, followed on Tuesday night by Chelsea at home and then on Sunday 23rd January we head to Leicester.

Nothing to fear there with Brighton putting such good results on the board. Well done lads – and up the Albion (the Brighton one).

Friday night proved that Brighton have the edge on Palace
January 15th 2022

Brighton 1 Crystal Palace 1

On another cold, dark and chilly evening, we found ourselves at the Amex again. Unlike for the past few home games, the atmosphere was electric as Crystal Palace came to town. By full time, we had seen that the Albion now have the edge over their rivals.

Brighton were so unlucky not to have the full three points, showing that they were the better team on the night. The table does not lie either and we sit four points above Palace. If it stays like that until the end of the season, nobody can deny that the Albion have overtaken Palace.

Having watched Palace the previous Saturday lunchtime against Millwall in the FA Cup on TV, it was clear that they would be a force to be reckoned with – even without three players including their club legend Wilfred Zaha who is at the African Cup of Nations.

The likes of Conor Gallagher, Michael Olise and Christian Benteke are all good players, and all were available to Patrick Viera on the night.

It was an early start for us from North Sussex on Friday afternoon. We boarded the Seagulls Travel coach from Lindfield having decided that it was the most sensible mode of transport as I did not feel that I wanted to be caught up with any Palace mobs on the train at my age of 66-years-old.

Some 40 minutes after leaving Lindfield, we cruised into the ground. Just like at the Arsenal game, there were buses and coaches in numbers you have never seen before.

Excitement was building and there was quite a backlog to get into the stadium. It was nice to get seated and when the team was announced, I counted seven changes from the side who played against West Brom in the FA Cup the previous week.

The Brighton bench looked particularly strong with a host of talent for Graham Potter to call upon as the game went on.

A few minutes before kick-off and the ground suddenly came alive. It was as if everyone drinking on the concourses had swallowed their pints in one gulp to dive into position ready to belt out Sussex By The Sea. The anthem was really sung with feeling and passion, the noise inside the stadium something else.

This atmosphere fed into a game which had it all. A missed penalty from Pascal Gross. A disallowed goal from Neal Maupay. Palace taking an underserved lead and then a late own goal to make it Brighton 1-1 Palace.

The Albion played a blinding first half in my opinion. As the game progressed, they settled down and really took it to the visitors.

A great move from the back led Jakub Moder to send a long ball forward. Although this was cut out, Marc Cucurella picked up the pieces, moving possession onto Leandro Trossard, who was away on goal with only Palace goalkeeper Jack Butland to beat.

Butland unfortunately made a great stop, and the Albion were denied an opening goal. The whole stadium was on its feet in response, a real sign of how much winning this game would mean.

Next, Alexis Mac Allister placed a beautiful corner into the penalty area. It Rick O'Shayed around before being hit over the bar by Moder.

Referee Robert Jones though was advised that there had been a possible infringement on Joel Veltman by Will Hughes. It turned out there was no possible about it… watching it back after and Hughes had wrestled Veltman to the ground.

Mr Jones gave the signal that Brighton were to have a penalty and the Amex erupted. Gross was the chosen taker and he missed with a very poor, weak penalty lacking substance or flair easily saved by Butland.

Actually, there was some flare – a big red one thrown onto the pitch as Gross prepared to take by the Palace fans behind the goal.

This delayed proceedings a little, which did not help Gross in the build-up. The flare also came very close to hitting Butland – only a Palace supporter would think it a good idea to hurl a lit flare at their own goalkeeper.

From the resulting corner, Gross' delivery made its way to the far post where Maupay bundled into the back of the net.

Another VAR review from Mr Jones saw him conclude that Maupay's left foot had been rather high when coming together with Butland, causing the ball to come loose from the Palace goalkeeper's arms.

The goal was disallowed and so it remained Brighton 0-0 Palace at half time. Brighton should have been a couple of goals ahead as Palace were unable to deal with the great football being played by the Albion.

I thought we might have seen Benteke come on at half time to try and help Palace record their first shot on target. That was not to be. Whatever Vieira what said during the 15-minute interval seemed to work however as Palace were a bit better in the second half.

Moder had another good chance deflected onto the cross bar before the game became more of an end-to-end contest, including Robert Sanchez making a good save from Odsonne Édouard.

It was Conor Gallagher who gave Palace the lead, slotting home in the 69th minute. Dan Burn did so well to nearly block the shot, coming close to getting a vital touch which would have diverted it away from goal. He was literally inches away… if only he had a few more on top of his existing 6'7.

Palace seemed to grow in confidence from taking the lead. Potter needed to do something, and he made changes, Danny Welbeck and Solly March joining Tariq Lamptey who had come on earlier in the second half.

The fresh legs provided new ideas as Brighton attacked the North Stand. With each passing minute though it appeared as if the game was going to end in defeat for Brighton.

Then with three minutes remaining, Maupay crossed to the near post from tightly on the touchline. Joachim Andersen tried to clear but only succeeded in diverting it past Butland to make it 1-1 right at the death.

There was still a chance for Brighton to win it. Welbeck took a great header which just skimmed over the bar from a March cross. You could argue that Lamptey should have had a penalty too when he was infringed but Mr Jones said no.

Alas, that was the end of the entertainment and with a little more luck, Brighton would have won. It looked like a large number of fans needed luck getting home in a safe and orderly manner too, a bit of a foo-pa taking place in leaving the ground which we luckily missed.

I am really looking forward to Chelsea on Tuesday night. Play like we did in the first half and it should be a cracking game – and a chance to move further ahead of Palace in the table.

Two home games in four days: Great excitement, even when you're 66
January 22nd 2022

Brighton 1 Chelsea 1

Here we went again! For the second time in four days, it was off to the Amex. The prospect of going to home matches in such quick succession never loses its excitement, even for a 66-year-old season ticket holder.

Conditions for the match against Chelsea were perfect. It didn't rain, the temperature was above freezing, and the scene was set for Brighton to cause more problems for the Champions of Europe.

Chelsea could have moved into second place with victory at the Amex. With the way that Thomas Tuchel had reacted to the 1-1 draw at Stamford Bridge last month, Brighton however had even more reason to make things difficult for the visitors.

True to form, Tuchel continued his grizzles again this time. He bleated on about having to play too many games. Compare that to our very own Graham Potter, who never moans. He and his squad just get on with the job.

How many of us thought as we entered the Amex, "Are we going to win tonight?" In my heart, it was going to finish 2-1 to the Albion – a prediction that might have seemed mad at the start of the season.

Not now though. There is always a possibility that this Brighton squad can win no matter the opposition, as they have shown on a regular basis.

I emphasises the word squad and not just team, because the depth we have to compete with so many players missing shows how the Albion are ever developing.

Seagulls Travel gave us another great ride to the stadium with time to spare. With a hotdog in one hand and a bag of Wine Gums from the Albion Sweet Shop in the other, it was time to take a seat in the East Upper.

Our normal neighbours were unable to make the game, meaning there was extra room to jump up and down if the occasion arose.

It did not take long for such an opportunity, an amazing bit of football getting Jakub Moder the first chance of the game. I was out of my seat, but it turned out prematurely; the ball fizzed just past the south goal, missing Kepa Arrizabalaga's post by inches.

You could tell from that start that the lads were up for it. They worked hard for each other, and the sense of togetherness was there for all to see, compared to Chelsea and their problems with Romelu Lukaku wanting away.

Chelsea remain a class team though. They drove forward and Cesar Azpilicueta found Robert Sanchez on his toes as Sanchez batted away a one handed save that he made look easy.

A short time later and Hakim Ziyech collected a short pass from N'Golo Kante. From outside the penalty area, Ziyech struck a shot towards Sanchez's near post.

I would bet that it caught Sanchez out as he was going the right way, only to be beaten low to the ground at his near post. We had been playing the better football, but a lucky shot suddenly had Chelsea one up.

The visitors nearly made it two a minute before half time. Callum Hudson-Odoi leathered way over the crossbar and into the North Stand, who made an incredible noise throughout the game. The atmosphere has been really good at both the Chelsea and Crystal Palace matches.

It was not long into the second half before Brighton began to peeper the Chelsea goal. Danny Welbeck started off proceedings but was just not able to get enough on an effort from a very tight angle on the left side.

More great play and real wizardry from Marc Cucurella and Dan Burn released Cucurella to play a nifty little chip back at the goal line.

Alexis Mac Allister met it but his shot was saved by Arrizabalga. I don't think that stop got the credit it deserved, taking a deflection off Jorginho and looking destined for the very bottom corner of the goal.

Mac Allister took the resulting corner and what a delivery it was. The ball was sent to the penalty spot where Adam Webster met it unmarked, squarely thumping the ball with his head into the Chelsea net.

It was a great, great goal, as good a set piece routine as you will see. And boy was it deserved. The whole stadium – except the 3,000 visitors of course – went berserk.

Webster celebrated in front of the North Stand and emotions were high as some youngsters began climbing the wall, which as we all know is big no-no.

Watching the highlights back and you can see the delight on Potter's face at his captain-for-the-night scoring. Leandro Trossard too looked so happy as he waited to be substituted on.

There were a full 30 minutes left to go and hopes were high Brighton could now go on and win the game. Trossard soon found his feet, using his technical skills to help Cucurella and Mac Allister move through Chelsea players with ease.

Another cross came in just missed by Neal Maupay. At this point, I am sure the players felt victory was within their grasp.

Chelsea though are not European Champions for nothing, and they finished the stronger, including when making one great opportunity which ended with a long shot from Marcos Alonso going over the bar.

From the 80th minute to the 94th, the Albion had to battle away as if all their lives were at stake. Chelsea brought on Timo Werner with Tommy Tucker… sorry, Thomas Tuchal doing all he could to urge his side to find a winner.

The Blues could not get there though. The applause and cheering afterwards reflected what a great effort it was from the Albion to hold the Champions of Europe for the second time in three weeks.

Webster and Dan Burn in particular earned their applause. Webster I am sure will be in the sights of Gareth Southgate, not just for his defending but the way he glides past opposition players so easily.

Burn's job meanwhile was to stick with Lukaku all the time. When Lukaku gets going, he can be like a Sherman Tank charging down the pitch. Burn was spot on in preventing that ever happening, providing a real helping hand.

It is a privilege to watch Brighton at the moment. The hard graft is paying off and is an absolute credit to the players, Potter, and the management team. Leicester City – you're next!

Hide behind the settee Sunday until Lamptey and Welbeck turned it around
January 22nd 2022

Leicester 1 Brighton 1

The lucky ones were off to the King Power Stadium to see Brighton take on Leicester. For the rest of us, it was listening to BBC Radio Sussex from the warmth of our homes – an experience also forced upon Graham Potter and Billy Reid.

Okay, so they were probably linked up to the game via some sort of feed and not relying on Johnny Cantor and Warren Aspinall to describe what was going on.

First team coach Bjorn Hamberg took charge in the absence of Graham and Billy, ably assisted by Bruno sitting right alongside him in a situation that was quite unexpected after both the Albion's manager and assistant were struck down with Covid-19.

It just goes to show that Covid is still out there, and we must all still take some precautions. I could not help but wonder though if Potter's settee springs would take the same sort of bashing mine have when celebrating at home moments in matches, I have been unable to attend?

Pre-game thoughts about Graham's settee turned out to be a case of counting chickens before they had hatched. There was no chance of any springs taking a bashing at the homes of Brighton fans listening in as it instead turned out to be a first half spent hiding behind the settee with Leicester being much the better side.

The Albion struggled to string together those wonderful passing moves we have seen of late. Johnny and Warren told us after 28 minutes that Brighton's passing had been very ragged with a tone of concern regular listeners know we have hardly heard so far this season.

It sounded as though Brighton were just not at it in the first half. You wondered how long before Hamberg turned to the bench, where Tariq Lamptey and Danny Welbeck sat along with Lewis Dunk, in the Albion squad for the first time in six weeks. It is great to know that our captain fantastic will be back on the pitch very soon.

A rare moment of Brighton excitement occurred in the one minute of first half stoppage time. The front line of Leandro Trossard and Neal Maupay combined with Trossard crossing to his partner who unfortunately did not find the back of the net.

There was a certain sigh of relief at going into the break at 0-0. Did Potter feel the same as he went to make himself a cup of tea at half time, before hopefully having a word with the squad via Zoom?

If Potter did speak to the players than whatever he said did not appear to work. The whistle went to restart the game, the ball bounced around the Albion's half for no more than 30 seconds and Paston Daka ended up putting it into the back of the net.

The Albion were 1-0 down before a lot of fans would have had the opportunity to even take their place on (or behind) the settee.

It is quite incredible how this squad do not ever give up. They knew they had been bad in the first half. They knew they had made a poor start to the second. And yet they continued to drive on.

Alexis Mac Allister popped one over the bar. Then came the changes as off went Pascal Gross and Steve Alzate to be replaced by Welbeck and Lamptey.

When you have two players of the quality of Welbeck and Lamptey who can come onto the turf, then you know that it is never over. Brighton possess subs who can make a difference.

It was not long before Lamptey's wizardry was showing, and Welbeck became the first Brighton player to really test Kasper Schmeichel with a header from his fellow substitute's cross.

Brighton kept pushing and it paid off. Maupay placed a pinpoint ball onto Welbeck's head, and he powered past Schmeichel, making it 1-1 with yet another goal in the final 10 minutes of a game.

Unlike some of those recent late equalisers against West Ham, Southampton and Chelsea, there were enough minutes left on this occasion to push for victory.

Dan Burn thought he had given it to Brighton. Another great corner from Mac Allister was headed towards goal and seemed to be going into the left corner until Youri Tielemans cleared off the line. Watching back the highlights, you could see what a great attempt it was from Burn.

With Solly March also on and delivering testing crosses, Brighton were first to everything. If anyone was going to win it from that point, it was the Albion.

"Careful, Tony" I said to myself when bouncing up and down on the settee. By now I was too excited to give much thought to what was happening to the furniture in the Potter household.

That big chance to secure victory came right near the end. March put in another cracking ball and Trossard hit an unbelievable shot kept out by an even better Schmeichel save.

The stop from the Leicester captain ensured it finish Leicester 1-1 Brighton. In the end, a fair result probably as both teams had their time on top.

Brighton though where a different outfit in the second half. If we can take that into out next game at Spurs in the FA Cup on February 5th, then who knows what can happen at the Tottenham Hotspur Stadium?

Let us hope the players enjoy their rest, Graham and Billy recover soon and this wonderful fighting spirit from the squad continues. Up the Albion!

How many Premier League CEOs can you ask about a blocked toilet?
January 28th 2022

Fans Forum

There are not many Premier League football clubs who allow you to sit in the comfort of your own home and directly ask the Deputy Chairman questions.

Which is what makes the semi-regular Brighton & Hove Albion Fans' Forum such a good occasion. The January 2022 event was held online with Paul Barber joined by Head of Supporter Services Jenny Gower and Head of Media and Communications Paul Camillin.

Mr Barber took every question very seriously, giving full and detailed answers throughout the session which lasted two hours.

It was a real eye opener into the sort of difficult decisions the club have to make and how careful those in charge must be to ensure it is run successfully.

Take the decision on the FA Cup allocation for Spurs away. The club could have ended up squandering £50,000 on tickets which went unsold, leaving them out of pocket.

Listening to the Fans' Forum left me absolutely convinced that the pyramid of senior managers and support staff off-the-pitch is every bit as good as Graham Potter and the players on it.

These people will continue to take Brighton forward in an era that we as Albion fans should feel extremely lucky to be a part of. My late dad would have loved it!

Mrs Gower started off by saying that the Fans' Forum coincided with the launch of the new Fan Advisory Board idea. This would see a group of elected representatives from across the supporter base meet with club officials to discuss issues.

The finer details are still being worked out and an announcement would follow later in the year. We already have one of the most open board-fan relationships in the Premier League and this will grow it further.

I was unsure how long the session would last so I jumped in early to ask Mr Barber three questions. My first was about attendance figures and the discrepancy between what the club announces and how many people are actually at the Amex.

Mr Barber explained that the club reports tickets sold and that this is not necessarily the actual number of people inside the stadium. This is per the request of the Premier League.

My second question was the most important. I asked on behalf of my good lady wife and all the other ladies who sit in the East Upper why the toilets have been continually blocked at almost every game this season.

This is not a pleasant experience for our female fans. Mr Barber said he would get David Baker to look into the problem.

So, there we have it ladies, let us hope Mr Baker can sort the blockage out and improve your toilet experience for the remaining home matches.

My final question was about car parking and the loss of Bennett's Field. Mr Barber explained quite clearly that Mr Bennett wants to build on his land rather than rent it to the Albion again.

University accommodation was mentioned and so it seems unlikely that Brighton fans will be able to use the car park again anytime soon. The club are mindful of the problems this is causing and have the situation under constant review.

Other subjects raised included the season ticket sharing scheme. Mrs Gower sought to explain to those who were confused about how it worked, as well as laying out the changes announced as part of the 20022-23 season ticket renewal package announced earlier in the week.

Another supporter asked about the increase of violence at the Amex and more pitch invasions taking place. The answer to that was the club have a duty of care to protect their staff and anybody who threatens that by getting onto the pitch will not be allowed back.

The club said they have been looking at the issue of safe standing. Chelsea and Spurs are amongst the Premier League clubs now offering it.

Mr Barber said that the Amex had never been built withstanding in mind. If seats were removed to accommodate the space needed for safe standing, then revenue would drop.

The Albion have lost money through having their doors shut during the pandemic and any businessman must therefore be careful about how they steer their business through many more difficult months.

It is no good getting everything right on the pitch, but then making foolish decisions behind the scenes. When you read about Derby County, it is easy to understand that viewpoint.

The Rams are on the brink of being closed due to a lack of money caused by terrible decision making in the boardroom. They are a famous, well supported, and traditional club who have a fantastic stadium. If it can happen to them, it can happen to anyone.

I must say that the two hours spent listening to senior figures at the club was extremely enlightening. They clearly have supporters at the heart of what they do, so let us help and put our faith behind them when tough decisions have to be made.

It was an enjoyable evening and I felt extremely privileged to be able to take part. Up the Albion – and here is to a working ladies toilet in the East Upper.

Out of the FA Cup – but Brighton know they can take points from Spurs
February 9th 2022

Spurs 3 Brighton 1

The run up to Brighton's FA Cup tie at Spurs was largely dominated by fans moaning about the ticket allocation. The Albion took 5,700 tickets out of a possible 9,000 and this seemed to upset a lot of people.

Whilst it is true that we have seen in recent times nearly 7,000 away fans go to MK Dons when increased allocations have been offered, that was for a 3pm kick off on a Saturday. There were trains running, parking near the stadium and Brighton were going for promotion.

Spurs away was different. Line repairs meant you could not get the train home afterwards and there is nowhere to leave a car close to the Tottenham Hotspur Stadium.

No sensible businessperson would gamble on buying 9,000 tickets and risk losing £50,000 if they did not sell out. Thankfully, our club is run by sensible business people.

Once the weekend rolled around, those gripes about tickets could not distract from the business of the FA Cup. What a weekend it was for it.

Kidderminster Harriers were unlucky not to pull off one of the greatest shocks ever at home to West Ham, where they led 1-0 until the 91st minute only to lose 2-1 in the last minute of extra time. How unfortunate for the non-league side.

We also saw good old Middlesbrough take out Manchester United 8-7 on penalties. Chris Wilder must have been so proud of his team's efforts.

Of interest for Brighton fans at Old Trafford was Aaron Connolly coming on to chase shadows in the second half. You thought there might have been a chance for him to shine when it went to penalties, but even as the shoot-out went to sudden death he still did not feature.

Is there some clause that means loanees are not eligible to take spot kicks in the FA Cup which I did not previously know about?

Unfortunately, Brighton were not able to join Middlesbrough in the next round. With the way the squad has been performing lately, I think a lot of us felt there was a good chance we could take out Spurs. But we also thought it would have to be a good day with no howling errors.

Needless to say, it was not one those days. To quote our amazing coach Graham Potter, "We were not at our best."

Which was in stark contrast to the Tottenham Hotspur Stadium, which most first-time visitors from Brighton described as the best in England.

I also learnt that it is apparently the greenest not only in this country, but in the whole of Europe. Don't tell Brighton City Council that as they might get a little upset.

For those who did not get a ticket, the game was televised on ITV4. Our ambassador in the studio was Glenn Murray, along with former Spurs player Robbie Keane.

It still bugs me that whenever Brighton are shown live, the market share of coverage always goes to the other team.

Spurs this, Spurs that... poor Glenn did his best to get a word in for Brighton, but it was just so one sided that neutrals might have forgotten two teams were playing.

Brighton started well enough, moving the ball around well. There was an early warning sign of what was to come however when Harry Kane could not make the most of a dodgy clearance from Robert Sanchez and the Albion were lucky to escape a calamity.

Then within seconds, poor Adam Webster stumbled when trying to decide whether to clear the ball up the right or run with it.

Before Webster knew what had happened, Son Heung-min was on the ball and slipping a pass to Pierre-Emile Hojbjerg. Next the ball went to Harry Kane who was not correctly marked, allowing him to take on two defenders and rocket a shot into the top corner.

It was an amazing strike and a great goal. Brighton though were guilty of making mistakes and you cannot do that at this level, as the players well know.

A slice of fortune gave Spurs their second. Solly March kept pace with Emerson Royal running down the right, only for the Albion player to deflect a cross high and fast over the head of Sanchez and into the back of the net for 2-0 to Spurs.

This was bad luck for Brighton, but it just goes to show how many problems deflected balls and crosses can cause for goalkeepers and defenders – as Spurs would discover themselves a little later.

Half time was reached with the Albion 2-0 behind and facing an uphill climb to get back into the game. Brighton came out full of enthusiasm after Potter's team talk, the players probably angry with themselves for what had happened in the first half and showing that fighting spirit the Albion have become known for.

Spurs had plenty to think about, especially from Yves Bissouma. He was simply amazing. There was a back heel in the area for Neal Maupay to do a quick turn which was unfortunate not to lead to a goal.

Maupay seemed to snatch at the chance, and one would think he would be disappointed not to really test Hugo Lloris.

Jakub Moder was next to be disappointed when sending one too high. Bissouma had a shot tipped over as the game opened up, but that let Spurs show their might on the counter and Sanchez did well to save from Son and Kane.

Then it happened. Bissouma got the goal he deserved, coming across towards the right side of the Spurs goal, working his way back across into more space and hitting a shot which deflected off Hojbjerg.

Now the fight back could begin. Or so we thought. Brighton being within one goal of Spurs was short lived, Son ran from almost the halfway line, going past Webster and Lewis Dunk at speed.

Sanchez came out to challenge and ended up being beaten by Webster of all people who knocked the ball past his own goalkeeper. Webster chased back to try and retrieve the situation, but Kane slid in to make it Spurs 3-1 Brighton.

I always say, "It is never over until the fat lady sings" and the Albion might have made a game of it if Maupay had finished a gem of a pass from Webster.

Maupay though could only put his shot straight at Lloris who comfortably made the save, another chance that Neal knew got away.

Substitute Danny Welbeck also came close with a header that fizzed wide whilst for Spurs, Steven Bergwijn ballooned a sitter over the bar after Antonio Conte gave the Albion some relief by taking off Son.

This may not have been the Albion's night but think about this – it can serve as a base for Brighton to go onto take six points from Spurs in the Premier League in the two meetings still to come this season.

Potter and the players now have a better idea of the current Spurs set up under Conte and they will surely not make the same individual mistakes next time they face Tottenham. The Albion's exit from the FA Cup can yet be turned into a positive.

Goal on the watch but not on the radio: The pitfalls of listening to Brighton online
February 12th 2022

Watford 0 Brighton 2

For the Watford v Brighton game, I decided to change things up a bit and listen to BBC Radio Sussex via the Albion website rather than through the wireless.

This was to hopefully ensure a good, uninterrupted commentary. And for 80 of the 90 minutes, it worked. The sound quality was so clear you could hear the wind from Vicarage Road.

Unfortunately, the clearness of listening over the internet comes at a price – a significant time delay. As the game ticked into the 82nd minute and Johnny Cantor and Warren Aspinall were praising a good bit of Watford defending, my watch buzzes with an alert: Brighton goal.

Hang on a minute, they have not even taken the corner on the radio. I waited, waited, waited, waited… and then Adam Webster scored in a goalmouth scuffle. Brighton led Watford 2-0 and all three points were as good as in the bag.

When having to wait three minutes to find out how the Albion scored their second goal is the biggest gripe of the afternoon, you know it has been a good day.

The sun shone both in Sussex and Watford. Adrian Charms, Johnny and Warren said before the game that they needed sunglasses to see what was going on. Watching the highlights back, even Roy Hodgson needed a cap to keep the sun out of his eyes.

Watford's traditional theme music of Z Cars greeted the teams onto the pitch. There was a surprise in the starting XI with Yves Bissouma and Leandro Trossard left on the bench and Graham Potter instead starting Danny Welbeck and Adam Lallana.

Johnny and Warren were impressed by the Albion's positive start, including an early corner that came to nothing.

I read somewhere recently that a corner coach now sits on the Brighton bench to help out with set pieces. Maybe this is why we have looked so dangerous from corners and free kicks in recent months?

Jakub Moder had a good chance but as has been the case throughout his Albion career so far, he could not find the back of the net.

It will surely not be long before Moder puts the ball in the onion bag, to coin a favourite phrase of Mr Aspinall.

Neal Maupay was then given too much space by the Watford defence, and he took a cracking early shot saved by Ben Foster.

Brighton had nearly all the possession in the first half. There was only one heart-in-mouth moment when Watford's Emmanuel Dennis broke down the right after Joel Veltman lost possession.

It sounded as if Dennis was on an express train the speed he was going and when watching it back it looked that way too.

When Dennis burst inside, Lewis Dunk intercepted to prevent the shot. Dunk must have clipped Dennis however as referee Jonathan Moss awarded a free kick right on the edge of the box. Dennis took it but thankfully put it wide right of the Albion goal.

Brighton got their break in the 44th minute when Tariq Lamptey crossed from the right and Maupay caught the ball with a right foot volley.

The ball defied the swirling wind and went straight into the back of the net. It sounded great on the radio – with no watch spoilers – and was even more spectacular when watched back.

Maupay is now level as the leading Albion goal scorer in the Premier League alongside the legend Glenn Murray – not bad company for a striker to be in.

Dennis continued to be Watford's biggest threat in the second half. It looked like he would score when running past a couple of Brighton defenders only to hit the crossbar.

Watford did seem more organised, but they were also becoming frustrated. A seething chop on Lamptey earned Hassane Kamara a yellow card. Lamptey did not appear injured, thank God.

The opportunities seemed to be coming thick and fast now on the radio, the result being my cup of tea getting slopped all over the shop with excitement.

Oh, for this run of four consecutive away games to be over so we can all get back to the Amex for Burnley – even if there are no trains heading south to Brighton. My settee needs a rest, and I can't keep spilling tea.

Marc Cucurella had a shot saved by Foster and then it was Moder's turn to be denied again. What does he have to do score?!

And then came the watch alert. Webster had fired in a rebound with his left foot over Foster and high into the roof of the Watford net.

Watford managed to muster one more chance after Brighton went 2-0 ahead, Ismaila Sarr having a shot safely dealt with by Robert Sanchez.

The full-time whistle then blew over the radio, meaning the action at Vicarage Road had probably finished five minutes ago.

Another clean sheet and another three points set us up nicely for Tuesday night's trip to Manchester United, where the radio will again keep me up to date – although maybe not listening through the internet this time!

On a final note, I really enjoyed watching Newcastle number 33 Big Dan Burn make his debut for his boyhood club against Aston Villa on Sunday afternoon.

Burn gave a performance worthy of the Sky Sports Man-of-the-Match award as Newcastle beat Villa 1-0. You could see how much it meant to him, and it is great to see him making a real impression right away.

Up the Burn and Up the Albion!

Surround the referee, get a player sent off: The Manchester United way
February 17th 2022

Man Utd 2 Brighton 0

A Tuesday evening, new batteries in the wireless and the anticipation that Brighton could go and win at Manchester United. The last part may not have happened, but the Albion played exceptionally well at Old Trafford.

Unfortunately, we as a club know all too well that a good performance does not always mean a good result. Graham Potter tells us that on a regular basis and once again it came true in his 100th game in charge of Brighton.

You felt the players would want to mark the milestone in style for what Potter has done for them and the Albion. They certainly put up a good fight.

It was very frustrating that despite this being a game between two prominent teams sitting fifth and ninth before kick-off, we were unable to watch it live on television.

There was plenty on the line after all; a United win would lift them into the Champions League places. If the Albion were lucky enough to pick up three points, they would climb to eighth at the same time as taking a first ever victory at Old Trafford.

Potter's starting XI showed three changes from Watford with Tariq Lamptey, Adam Lallana and Danny Welbeck dropping out for Yves Bissouma, Alexis Mac Allister, and Leandro Trossard.

The media have been going on and on non-stop about United in the run-up to the game and not much of it positive coverage.

This must have left United's players feeling under pressure and negative and I began to think to myself that maybe Potter and the Albion would look to harness that to their advantage.

They appeared to do so in the first 30 minutes. Backed by a noisy Seagulls following who could be heard loudly on BBC Radio Sussex, it was all Brighton according to the commentary from Johnny Cantor and Warren Aspinall.

Jakub Moder sounded like he was in the thick of things. He had a good chance when Pascal Gross crossed and then an even better one with a header from a Joel Veltman cross.

I was already out of my seat as the tone of the radio made it sound as if there was no way Moder's powerful effort could be kept out.

The settee springs ended up taking one of their biggest bashings of the season as I crashed back down to the news that David De Gea had somehow made the save.

I must have watched it back about 20 times and how De Gea stopped it, I will never know. It was a save that has to be seen to be believed and it of course had to be from poor Jakub, whose wait for a Premier League goal goes on.

Yves Bissouma had a sight of goal before half time after a classy move from Brighton, but his shot was just wide. It is good to see Bissouma shooting from distance again, his faith appearing to have been boosted by that goal at Spurs in the FA Cup.

0-0 and looking the better, more organised team was a good way for the Albion to go into the break. If they could keep up that tremendous pace in the second half, then we would have a chance.

Unfortunately, those hopes took a blow when Bissouma had a rare moment of losing possession. That gave United the ball and Cristiano Ronaldo had a run and shot which ended with him putting his side 1-0 ahead. "BUM" I thought.

Then came the game's turning point. Lewis Dunk challenged Anthony Elanga and they both went down outside the penalty area.

Referee Peter Bankes immediately went for his yellow card which looked the right decision as Adam Webster was covering behind and so it could not be seen as a clear goal scoring opportunity.

Not that United agreed. Suddenly, Mr Bankes was surrounded by a red wolf pack who looked like they were going to tear his throat out if he gave anything less than a red.

Ronaldo was at the front giving it the big one when he was not even involved in the incident. Mr Bankes touched his ear. I think all the commotion forced him to go to the monitor and as everyone knows, it is never good when that happens.

A message must have flashed up on the screen: "Anything you can do to help Man United please do so." Mr Bankes ran back onto the pitch and showed Dunk the red card.

United had bamboozled the referee into making an incorrect decision that paid no attention to the position of Webster.

The antics of those players in red was embarrassing. If Brighton had behaved as badly to the referee, then they would have had a player sent off and rightly so.

If United thought it would be easy from now on, they were mistaken. The Albion might have been 1-0 behind and down to 10 men but they never give up.

Brighton went on the attack when they had the chance, causing United problems. Robert Sanchez meanwhile deserved a medal for the saves he was making at the other end to keep us in the game.

Three or four amazing stops in the final 15 minutes forgave him from the one moment he faltered with a clearance. There was nothing he could do about the two goals, Bruno Fernandes making it Man United 2-0 Brighton in the last seconds on the counterattack.

Defeat was not a fair result in my opinion, but we can take heart that this Albion team have shown that they can beat United on a level playing field.

Take away incorrect red cards and penalties awarded after the final whistle and Brighton are the better team. Maybe United know this and that is why they celebrated afterwards like they had just won the FA Cup, rather than beating 10 men?

Brighton blown away by Burnley, but season remains on track
February 19th 2022

Brighton 0 Burnley 3

Trees and bins were not the only things blown away by the worst storm Sussex had seen for 30 years – the footballers of Brighton & Hove Albion found themselves on the wrong end of a 3-0 defeat at the hands of Burnley.

It seemed like a long time since we had last visited the Amex for a home game and with the chaos caused by the weather, I did have my doubts about whether we would make it to the stadium.

There are rarely problems when Seagulls Travel are involved however, and they had us delivered to the Amex in perfect time for a pre-game meal of a lovely hotdog and a packet of Albion wine gums.

Burnley did not enjoy such a smooth journey. Their flight south was cancelled and so they had to make the trip via coach. Maybe their players wanting to stretch their legs after the long journey was why they ran rings around Brighton on the pitch?

The Clarets started the day bottom of the table in the relegation zone, as we all knew. Therefore, there was a natural expectation amongst supporters (and perhaps players) that Brighton should win the game.

Graham Potter knows better and he constantly alludes to there being no easy matches in the Premier League. The lower teams are desperately fighting for their survival and that is exactly how Burnley looked. They wanted it far more than the Albion.

A Brighton fan wrote on social media after the game that it looked like some sort of domestic had taken place in the Albion changing room even before Robert Sanchez and Shane Duffy had their little contretemps on the pitch.

Sometimes, emotions spill over. This is especially true when everyone is having a bad day at the office, as happens from time-to-time in all professions.

A bad day is exactly what Brighton 0-3 Burnley looked like for the Albion. Nothing more than that, and importantly the players have a chance to prove it in front of the Amex crowd straight away when Aston Villa come to town in a rare example of back-to-back home matches.

Potter and his coaching team will analyse what went wrong and as Adam Lallana said, everyone involved will learn from it. We all know this squad can play so much better than what they showed on Saturday.

The crucial thing for me is that we started the day in ninth place in the Premier League table and we finished the day in ninth place in the Premier League table.

We have to appreciate what the aim for this year was. I believe Tony Bloom wants to establish Brighton as a top 10 club, which we are still on target to achieve. The season remains on track even after a heavy defeat to Burnley.

Brighton are never going to win every game they play. Not even Manchester City do that, as we saw when they were beaten at home by Spurs.

Coming into the game, I felt the first goal was crucial. If we scored first, I was hopeful that confidence would soar, and we would go onto win by a decent margin. If we fell behind to opponents who needed three points so badly, then I worried we would be in trouble.

Burnley seemed to cope far better with the conditions in the first half when the wind swirled, and the rain poured.

We saw just how strong the wind was when Sanchez was stranded by a Connor Roberts effort which thankfully blew onto the top of the crossbar and behind for a goal kick.

The first Burnley goal came from good football finished off by new striker Wout Weghorst with a clinical finish that left Sanchez no chance.

In amongst all the doom and gloom, a lot of people have forgotten that Brighton rallied well after going behind. The stats showed the Albion dominating possession with some nice passing.

Jakub Moder had a decent effort and might have won a penalty when Aaron Lennon hauled him to the ground in the box.

Not for the first time, referee Kevin Friend was no friend of the Albion – even though watching the highlights back, it appeared that it took quite an effort from Lennon to bring Moder down.

A great passage of play ended with Lallana heading the ball just past the post in an example of another chance getting away from Brighton.

It was poor defending that gave Burnley their second, allowing Josh Brownhill to literally roll the ball into the goal, much to even the visiting player's surprise.

No doubt that it should have been prevented but with Duffy and Sanchez having already had their argument, this was turning into one of those days.

The second half started with a great Tariq Lamptey run down the East Stand touchline and an excellent volley attempt from Neal Maupay.

A difficult chance for the French striker, but one we have seen him score several times already this season. Alas, it was not to be against Burnley.

Lennon made it three shortly after, putting the ball in the top corner with another shot which Sanchez did not seem to have a chance with.

It was another great goal from Burnley, just kissing the underside of the bar as it went in. Undoubtedly, the sort of opportunity that our players should look back on and think we can do that as well.

We just couldn't do it against Burnley. Potter was not willing to blame Sanchez, Duffy, or any of his players for the poor display.

"I have to take the blame for today," he said afterwards, presumably talking about the formation which most pundits and Brighton fans pinpointed as the issue.

Time to put Burnley behind us and for Brighton to bounce back against Villa. Up the Albion.

Why come to the Amex to slag off a Brighton side sitting 10th in the Premier League?
February 26th 2022

Brighton 0 Aston Villa 2

On a beautiful February afternoon, the Amex was bathed in sunshine, and you could almost forget about the grim shadow hanging over the world at the current time.

We had a little longer than expected to enjoy the unseasonal weather before kick-off thanks to the Aston Villa team coach getting caught up in the traffic delays on the main roads approaching Brighton.

The Villa squad were not the only ones with travel issues. There were no trains again due to significant track repairs being carried out over nine consecutive days in an attempt to get the job done in one hit.

Not wanting to be stuck on a rail replacement bus down to Brighton, I opted to complete the journey via coach with Seagulls Travel. Once again, they got their beak to the forefront, and we got to the ground in very good time.

The previous week's 3-0 defeat to Burnley would no doubt have knocked the Albion's confidence. Back-to-back home games seemed to present a good opportunity to rebuild it and settle down to working once again as a team with the determination to stand their ground.

Since the Burnley game of course, war has begun in Europe and what is happening in Ukraine at present is a major worry for us all.

It serves as a reminder that a football result is an issue that in the grand scheme of things, we should not really take too much heart.

If anything, it should boost the regard that we hold our team in. They deserve our support, and we are lucky to be able to give it to them, whether they win or lose.

Some of us need reminding of this based on the reaction to Brighton 0-2 Aston Villa. Just because we lost against Villa, we should not be slagging off the squad on social media.

Watch back the highlights on Match of The Day and you will see that the Albion played a lot of good football. It was just one of those days when the chances that came Brighton's way would not go in the back of the net.

Compare that to the clinical finishing Villa produced. Matty Cash hit a good shot off Robert Sanchez's right-hand post for the opening goal on 17 minutes.

The defending might have been better as Cash appeared to have too much time and space. Even so, it was still a great strike that initially looked like it might be bending wide from the East Upper.

Cash stripped off his shirt in celebration and the usual yellow card took a little longer to come out from referee Jonathan Brooks.

The Villa man was eventually booked but the hesitancy from the referee became clear when watching the highlights. Cash had a message written to his friend Tomasz Kedzoria, who plays for Dynamo Kyiv. It said: "Stay strong bro". A sentiment we can all agree with.

Ollie Watkins scored Villa's second on 68 minutes. His was a fine finish too following a long ball over the top catching the Brighton defence out. It was Watkins' first goal in seven matches.

Alexis Mac Allister had the best chance for Brighton, but his shot kissed the top of the crossbar. There seemed to be a running set of disagreements between Cash and Emiliano Martinez all afternoon.

The Villa goalkeeper is a fine player and yet here he was being chastened on a number of occasions by his teammate. It was a shame Brighton could not test Martinez more to see if these arguments would impact on his game.

Nine yellow cards were shown throughout the 90 minutes, yes nine! It did get a little heated at times, leading to a feeling that the referee had lost control.

There was one shout in the second half from Tariq Lamptey that I felt really should have been looked at. This was not to be Brighton's day though.

Not that there is any shame in losing to Villa. Steven Gerrard won four of his first six matches remember and has his side defensively organised and playing with the sort of combative spirit he was known for as a player.

They were also backed by complete and unequivocal support. The noise coming from the South Stand was incredible against the very poor support from our own North Stand.

My little voice on its own in the East Upper just does not cut it. Everyone needs to work harder to improve the atmosphere at the Amex.

We must all give the lads 120 percent support whether they are winning or losing. It must give them such a lift when they can hear us even when the game is not going well.

Why come to the Amex to slag the players off? All that does is lower the tone. As a club, Brighton are still on target to finish 10th in the Premier League. How can people complain about that?

Of course, to maintain that top 10 position then Brighton need to start picking up points again soon. We tend to be better away from home this season and so hopefully the trip to Newcastle United will provide a chance to triumph.

Newcastle are showing real signs of improvement, including when beating Brentford 2-0 at the weekend. 90 minutes at St James' Park will not be easy, but Brighton have shown over most of this season what they can do. Up the Albion!

A Newcastle win and a happy Yodel delivery driver
March 5th 2022

Newcastle 2 Brighton 1

24 hours before Brighton kicked off away at Newcastle United and I met a couple of people in and around the village of Crawley Down who were in contrasting moods about the game at St James' Park.

One was an Albion fan who I accidentally bumped into on Friday night. He was travelling up by train the following morning on a return ticket costing in excess of £150 and a journey lasting many hours.

Our loyal away support really go above and beyond to follow the Albion around the country. Unfortunately, those costs are out of my budget and so I found myself keeping track from home.

You could certainly hear over the radio waves the 1,500 or so Brighton fans who had made the trip and were positioned in the seventh tier at St James' Park.

Newcastle put their away end up in the gods, so that the noise travelling supporters makes struggles to be heard on the pitch. If only we could do similar at the Amex, then the North Stand might find it easier to ousting the opposition.

Brighton fans will certainly need to be in good voice next week when Liverpool and their boisterous support visit.

The other person I met on Friday with an interest in the game was the local Yodel delivery driver. He is an avid Newcastle fan and had a ticket to the match, only to have been told that morning that he had to work on the Saturday as his stand-in had gone sick.

He was really upset to say the least, but still managed to grin after dropping off my parcel and wish Brighton luck with a strong hint of sarcasm in his voice.

I managed to resist slamming the door in his face by thinking the Albion would have the last laugh. How wrong can you be? Still, at least he would have been happy with the three points even if he had been unable to attend himself.

Fast forward to Saturday 2pm and the Brighton team was announced with a few surprises. Neal Maupay, Yves Bissouma, Alexis Mac Allister, Solly March and Adam Lallana were all on the bench.

Paul Merson on Soccer Saturday ran down Graham Potter for his selection, saying all those players had been left out as the Albion manager was playing a deliberately weakened team.

Merson obviously doesn't study the form before appearing on TV. Potter had to do something to try and end a run of three consecutive defeats.

Newcastle were seven without a loss, which the Albion might have been hoping would lead to some complacency. That did not work out, but the Magpies must be due a defeat soon surely?

A midweek clash with Southampton followed by Chelsea at the weekend will be worth keeping an eye on, otherwise my Yodel man is going to be even chirpier than normal.

St James' Park was stuffed to the gunnels with Ukraine flags, Newcastle Brown flags and the Magpies black and white flags. Tributes were paid before kick off to the suffering of Ukrainians at the moment and Brighton wore their yellow and blue kit in solidarity.

The message being sent was clear – football in England is thinking and saying prayers for them all. What is happening in Ukraine is truly unacceptable. I understand the situation even more now after watching a Netflix documentary called Winter on Fire.

I really do recommend it, however, please be aware there are some really upsetting scenes. It features real footage and has been made to highlight the troubled times when Ukrainians fought for their freedom not so long ago. Boy, do they have some determination as a country.

Back to the football and I tried something new this week, one ear on BBC Radio Sussex and the other ear on a computer screen. What the screen showed me in the first 10 minutes is that everything was going Brighton's way.

And then somehow in the space of two minutes, we were two goals behind. A good turn from Chris Wood saw him thread a ball through to Jacob Murphy who raced away.

Murphy really should have scored himself, but Robert Sanchez made himself big, forcing Murphy to put his shot against the post.

Unfortunately, it fell straight into the path of Ryan Fraser who slotted home with Joel Veltman unlucky not to block on the line.

Next a Fraser set piece found its way to the penalty spot where Fabian Scharr was on hand to head past Sanchez. Brighton now had a brick wall to climb, and the players could have been forgiven for looking a little deflated.

We saw in the Manchester Derby how quickfire goals can lead the floodgates to open. Roy Keane described how Manchester United gave up as being "unforgivable".

Giving up is something we rarely see from Brighton and at Newcastle, the Albion response was to keep plugging away and looking for opportunities.

It was another one of those days when chances just did not work out. Shane Duffy could tell you that even before Newcastle had taken the lead, his header from a great Pascal Gross corner was not-quite on target.

Dan Burn blocked a certain goal from Gross after Jakub Moder worked the ball beautifully around the home defence. Newcastle goalkeeper Martin Dubravka denied Danny Welbeck when pushing his shot over the ball after nice work by Tariq Lamptey.

Burn looked determined to make an impression at both ends and Sanchez was relieved to see his former teammate put a header just wide.

The man wearing orange in the Brighton goal next saved from Murphy as the sides went into half time with Newcastle leading 2-0.

Whatever the diagnosis and prescription offer by GP, it worked as the Albion were better in the second 45 minutes. A corner came Brighton's way in the 55th minute and a powerful header from captain Lewis Dunk made it 2-1. Game on.

The Albion went at Newcastle time and time again over the remaining 35 minutes. On came Maupay, March and Mac Allister to add fresh impetus.

Chances dropped for Maupay and Leandro Trossard. Dunk had another good header from a corner. The Albion kept going with no sign of any let up until the final whistle blew.

Had the game gone on for five or 10 minutes more, I am convinced it would have finished Newcastle 2-2 Brighton. However, we just ran out of time, and it was a fourth defeat in a row.

Where do we go from here? Onwards and very much upwards, certainly in terms of opponents from Newcastle near the bottom to title challenging Liverpool at the top.

Brighton drew with the Reds at Anfield earlier this season. We took four points from Jurgen Klopp last year. Give the team all the support we can and who knows what Saturday might bring? A less happy Yodel driver, hopefully. Up the Albion.

Should we be too downhearted after losing to one of the best in the world?
March 12th 2022

Brighton 0 Liverpool 2

What a beautiful day it was as Brighton were set to take on Liverpool. The sun was shining, there were blue skies everywhere and all was to play for at an Amex Stadium which looked even more amazing than normal.

Nearly as positive as the weather was the outlook of our Seagulls Travel coach driver. If the Albion could put in a performance to match his enthusiasm, then we would surely have no problems against Jurgen Klopp's Reds. Alas, it was not to be.

The visitors from Liverpool were in fine voice, almost as if they have been on an unbelievable run of form. And yes, they did steal one of our footballs during the game.

Did the referee add time on for that interruption? Probably not. It was a certain Mike Dean from the Wirral on Merseyside. He was also the man in the middle when Brighton drew 2-2 at Anfield in October.

I don't know what you think, but to have a neutral referee rather than one who lives a few miles away from the visitors would be nice. It would also stop any insinuations during and after the game that the officials are biased to their local club.

Certainly, Brighton fans did not feel that Mr Dean had given a fair performance if the reaction at full time was anything to go by.

The officials were booed off, which did seem a little harsh as they had kept Robert Sanchez on the pitch after a terrible challenge on Luis Diaz when Liverpool took the lead.

Before that happened, Brighton had begun strongly. Klopp said in his pre-match press conference that he likes the way Brighton play but does not enjoy the problems that it causes his side.

Klopp must have thought there would be plenty of problems again for Liverpool to deal with when Neal Maupay had an early shot not far away from Alisson's post.

Mo Salah and Sadio Mane then showed why they are such a dangerous combination when earning the visitors, a corner. That was a warning sign as Liverpool took the lead shortly after.

A long pass out of defence from Joel Matip headed towards Diaz, who was too quick for the Brighton defence to keep up with.

Diaz was brave and connected with a diving header even as the huge frame of Sanchez came flying through the air towards him. The ball rolled into the empty net as Sanchez connected with Diaz, the Liverpool forward going down like a sack of potatoes.

Sanchez had his head in his hands, suggesting that he thought a red card was coming. Going 1-0 down in the same instance as dropping to 10 men would have been a disaster for Brighton.

VAR took a look and decided it was accidental. Sanchez was allowed to carry on, a decision which basically every single pundit disagreed with.

It remained Brighton 0-1 Liverpool going into half time. Before the game, I felt that even if we went behind, we would still have a chance of getting back into it, providing we were clinical when chances came our way.

Very early in the second half and such an opportunity did fall to Brighton. A handball by Maupay in the build-up was missed by the officials – another reason they shouldn't have been booed – before Maupay laid off to Leandro Trossard. He skied it over and the Albion's second real chance of the game went begging.

Brighton were not the only ones showing wayward finishing. Diaz again used his pace to escape, this time from Joel Veltman and Tariq Lamptey.

He fed Salah who amazingly shot wide from the sort of position that he always scores. Lewis Dunk also deflected another Salah effort onto the bar. Maybe luck was on the Albion's side and Liverpool would not get a killer second?

That hope lasted for all of five minutes. Naby Keita took a shot which hit Yves Bissouma straight in the hand, right in front of Mr Dean.

A penalty was the only outcome and Salah made no mistake this time, driving down the middle as Sanchez dived the other way.

Even if Sanchez had saved it, a retake would have been likely. The Brighton goalkeeper was so far off his line that you could see it from the East Stand Upper.

Perhaps Ben Roberts and his coaching team should have a word, otherwise we may find ourselves in the position one day where Sanchez keeps a penalty out, only for it to be taken again.

It must be said that Brighton were better after going 2-0 down. Dunk hit a long ball for Lamptey to chase which Alisson came right to the edge of his area to gather.

Lamptey could not quite get there but as Alisson caught the ball, his momentum carried him outside the box. His feet left the area, but he twisted and held the ball inside with his outstretched arms.

Brighton fans and players wanted a free kick but no came the answer from Mr Dean. An interesting one and certainly something you do not see very often.

If Alisson had decided to handball it because he was bored, then he need not have bothered. The Albion ended up working in the Liverpool goalkeeper more in the final five minutes than they had in the 85 which had gone before.

Danny Welbeck forced a great, cat-like reaction save from Alisson and Solly March nearly capped a great personal game for himself with a consolation. A one-goal defeat rather than the two suffered would have been more justified on the balance of play.

Not that we should be too downhearted, anyway. Brighton were playing against one of the best teams in the world. They have huge amounts of cash and have been playing at the top level for many years.

It takes years a long time to reach that level. For a club who have only been in the Premier League five seasons, the Albion are not doing too bad in competing with teams like Liverpool.

Losing against Liverpool is not a problem; the results against Burnley and Aston Villa were more disappointing. Wednesday night sees Brighton take on another of the big clubs when Spurs come to the Amex.

Victory will be difficult. Perhaps though we can hope for a first home goal in a long time? Seeing Tottenham concede three times against Manchester United at the weekend makes me think our beleaguered forwards can profit.

I am convinced this run of defeats will end soon, providing we all get behind the players. It would be nice to do it against Spurs with another famous win at the Amex.

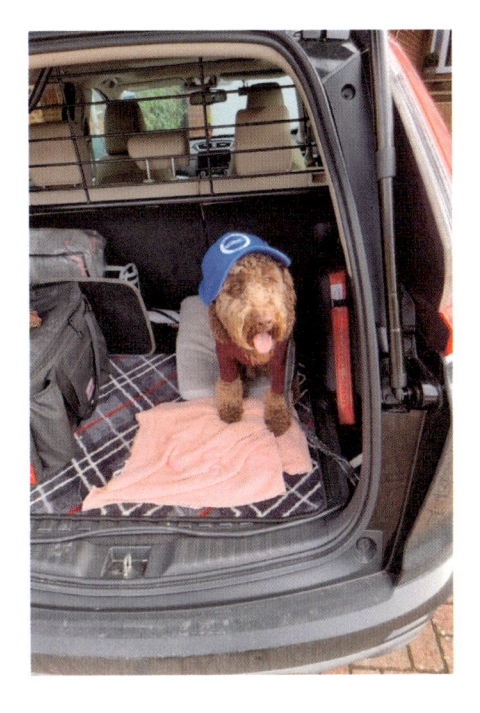

Good times or bad, we are all Brighton supporters, aren't we?
March 23rd 2022

Brighton 0 Spurs 2

When you are a true supporter of a football club, that support extends to the team through the good times and the bad. As Brighton fans, we know that better than most.

So, all the social media comments slagging the Albion off following the Spurs game made me wonder how true some of our supporters really are?

Yes, I understand the viewpoint and agree that these last six consecutive defeats have spoilt what had been a great start to the season.

We have to remember though that we are not ready yet for challenges like European football. The gradual build up to compete at that level regularly is what we need, rather than getting there before we are ready.

It takes many years to build a strong Premier League squad. Brighton have the potential to do that. Continuity and gradual investment are the key, something which the club will address this summer, I am sure.

We also need to show better support to the squad, especially at the Amex. There was one moment during Brighton 0-2 Spurs when the Albion were awarded a corner.

The crowd had gone quiet, and Leandro Trossard was forced into trying to gee everyone up. Away clubs who visit us do not need their players to encourage fans to cheer their team and Spurs were the latest visiting group of fans to make more noise than our own.

Even in these periods of bad results which are to be expected, we know our team will fight to the bitter end and never give up.

The players must be hurting and feeling pretty low at present, which is why having the fans behind them has never been more important than at this moment in time. Who knows what they can achieve with a passionate, supportive crowd?

Everton beating Newcastle United 24 hours after the Albion's defeat to Spurs was 100 percent evidence of this. It was a scrappy game for much of the 114 minutes – yes, 114 minutes.

The lengthy additional time was needed due to some young person cable tying themselves to the goalpost around their neck.

Both teams worked hard, including our former defender Dan Burn. One piece of class football from Dominic Calvert-Lewin and Alex Iwobi created a brilliant goal to put Everton 1-0 ahead with two minutes left to play.

Goodison Park is an old-school football ground like the Goldstone used to be. It was rocking when Everton scored, the noise pouring out of all three home stands amazing.

Everton fans know how to support their team, as we know from when they visited the Amex earlier in the season. They help carry their players over the line and for all Frank Lampard has done in football, I am sure he will never forget that moment of passion at Goodison.

An Everton win also did Brighton a bit of a favour, stopping Newcastle overtaking us. We hold onto 13th spot in the Premier League table ahead of the international break, giving the players time to rest and put all negative thoughts behind them to come out all guns blazing against Norwich.

I must admit I had a lot of those negative thoughts before the Spurs game, which makes you wonder if the players did too?

Brighton started well but there were still signs of nervousness from Robert Sanchez. Once again, Sanchez left it too late to clear when the ball was at his feet.

Thankfully for the Albion's young goalkeeper, Harry Kane missed the tap in he had been presented with from a tight angle.

Lucky Sanchez – and lucky Spurs when the visitors took the lead. Dejan Kulusevski put a shot towards goal which Sanchez might have saved had it not glanced off Christian Romero on the way through.

Kulusevski was looking good, and we got to see the better side of Sanchez's game when he made the save after the Swede put another shot on goal from a breakaway.

It was the sort of chance Spurs normally always score, so it was to the Albion's credit that the danger had been averted.

Half time arrived with Brighton 1-0 behind, just as they had been in the weekend defeat to Liverpool. The Albion's play had not been bad in the first 45 minutes.

If they could improve in the final third and be a bit more clinical, then the chance of getting a result still remained.

Brighton pressurised Spurs early on. The visitors looked a little unstable and panicky at the back. There was a shout for handball which was denied, and Alexis Mac Allister was fouled by Romero. The free kick from that led directly to a corner which the Albion could not do anything with.

Then came a sucker punch. Spurs broke on the counter; the ball was fed through to Kane. Sanchez looked a little hesitant, obviously thinking that he better not take out the England captain as he had against Luis Diaz in the Liverpool game. That left Kane with the simple task of rolling the ball past Sanchez and into the empty net.

Brighton players felt that Kane was offside. VAR checked and decided there was no case to answer. Sanchez then had to make a vital stop after a run by Sergio Reguilon and a one-two between Danny Welbeck and Neal Maupay looked like it might give Spurs something to worry about.

The Albion though could find no answer to Kane, who was having one of those evenings. Sanchez made another great save when Pierre-Emile Hojbjerg slipped in Kane and Shane Duffy was lucky to get away without conceding a penalty after a tackle on Kane, even though VAR took a look.

And so we all left the Amex feeling low again. On another day however, Brighton supporters know we can get a result. Payback against Spurs will not have to wait long as we play them again at the Tottenham Hotspur Stadium on April 16th.

Time to put the international break to good use and come back recharged against Norwich, ready to cheer the players to a first goal at the Amex since January 18th. Up the Albion!

Might some Seagulls luck end this scoreless rut?
April 2nd 2022

Brighton 0 Norwich 0

After a long 16-day break owing to internationals and Brighton being knocked out of the FA Cup by Spurs, the Albion returned to action against bottom of the table Norwich City looking to end their run of six consecutive defeats in which they had only scored once.

Not every Seagull was treated to a fortnight off, of course. Some represented their countries, a source of pride for both them and Brighton fans.

Players like Alexis Mac Allister, Leandro Trossard, Shane Duffy, and Jakub Moder all performed well on international duty.

There was also Andi Zeqiri, currently on loan at Augsburg in Germany. He played for Switzerland against England, showing Albion supporters what he can do live on national television from Wembley.

The hope had to be that those who had gone away would return with their confidence boosted and ready to get Brighton out of their rut.

Graham Potter said in his press conference before the game that the players who had remained in Brighton had benefited from the rest and that the coaching staff had used the 16 days well to get across ideas and improve the recent form.

Despite the promising words of Potter, I was sceptical. We all know the Albion like to do things the hard way, and so my bet was that we would draw with Norwich before beating Arsenal and taking a point from both Spurs and Manchester City.

With it finishing Brighton 0-0 Norwich, so far, I am onto a winner. The only problem being I am not a gambling man!

The Albion might not have been able to improve their record in front of goal, but one thing which has improved over the international break is the speaker system at the Amex.

It was so loud in the East Upper before the game that nobody could hear themselves think. I thought to myself that if the football was as good as the revamped PA, then we would be in for a treat.

And in a way, it was. Brighton created lots of opportunities and played some great stuff. They just had another of those days where the luck you sometimes need to score goals was not there.

The way Norwich set up made this like a game of bagatelle at times. Brighton were the billiards balls trying to find a way through and Norwich were 10 orange pins doing everything to protect their own goal.

If the Albion had a player called Rick O'Shea, maybe they would have found a way through. So many Premier League teams of late seem to get lucky with deflected goals, something which never happens to Brighton.

That is what we need to end this scoreless rut and with it, win a game. Once we get a piece of luck to break the duck, I have no doubt that more goals will follow, confidence will return and that we can start putting points on the board – even against the quality opposition Brighton face in their next three games on the road.

A nifty move and cross just eluded Danny Welbeck in front of the South Stand in the opening exchanges. Mac Allister then showed that he has been buoyed by playing alongside Lionel Messi for Argentina when firing not far wide of Tim Krul's left hand post.

The best opportunity Brighton had came from the penalty spot. Pascal Gross crossed, and a Norwich defender raised his arm right above his head to produce the clearest handball you will ever see.

The only conclusion I could reach for as to why the Norwich player had done it was that he was trying to keep the sun out of his eyes as the ball came into the box.

It was an easy penalty decision and yet it took an age from the offence taking place for the spot kick to be taken. In that time, Krul was able to walk up to Neal Maupay several times, delaying the kick further in an attempt to put Maupay off his stroke.

Not very sportsmanlike in my opinion but it worked. Maupay skied the penalty right over the bar. A golden opportunity which did not even hit the target, you cannot write this sort of stuff. It reaffirmed by view that we are going to end this run the hard way.

The crowd were at least supportive of Maupay when he was substituted in the second half. The North Stand sang his name as he walked around the pitch. That should at least give Maupay some confidence.

There cannot be any doubt that Brighton need to vary their strike force this summer however, a fact that Johnny Cantor and Warren Aspinall highlighted on BBC Radio Sussex and the Match of the Day pundits agreed with on Saturday night.

I would bet on Brighton getting some goal scorers in soon – although again, I am not a gambling man!

At half time, it was clear that the Albion would need only one goal to win the game. Norwich were not interested at all in venturing into the Brighton half.

The second 45 minutes saw the Albion have even more chances than in the first. So, so many chances. The breakthrough though never came. It was one of those days where nobody could get the ball in the onion bag, as Aspinall would say.

Watch the extended highlights and any disbeliever in this Brighton squad will see that the Albion have what it takes to start scoring and winning again soon.

Arsenal, Spurs and Manchester City are all difficult away games, but we have tended to play better against the stronger teams. A change of luck, a fortunate deflection and Brighton can get back on track. Up the Albion and keep the faith.

A Brighton win, a Grand National win, but what about the lottery?
April 9th 2022

Arsenal 1 Brighton 2

This has been quite the week in the Noble Household. Brighton won, the Grand National took place and I ventured cautiously into the world of online gambling with fantastic consequences.

Following last week's 0-0 draw with Norwich City, I wrote this: "We all know that Albion like to do things the hard way, and so my bet was that we would draw with Norwich before beating Arsenal and taking a point from both Spurs and Manchester City. With it finishing Brighton 0-0 Norwich, so far, I am onto a winner. The only problem being I am not a gambling man."

That last part is no longer true. On Saturday morning, I decided that my wife and I should have a little flutter on the Grand National to the tune of a £5 each way bet.

Having mastered the Albion website and season tickets on mobile phones, my newly installed Ladbrokes App was a walk in the park.

There was only one small matter of confusion, when I was asked if I wanted to boost my bet. Not being a gambling man, I had no idea what this meant so I just pressed the button which said yes.

The app then informed me I now had odds of 50/1 on the horse I had chosen, which of course had to be Noble Yeats. Should my prediction about the Albion winning at Arsenal not end up being correct, then at least there was the big race at Aintree to enjoy shortly after the final whistle.

Turned out I need not have worried. Brighton were magnificent at the Emirates, running out 2-1 winners. The finishing in front of goal from Leandro Trossard and Enock Mwepu was clinical.

The players can now go to Spurs next week with nothing to fear and confidence restored after a great shift was put in by all concerned.

Listening on the radio to Johnny Cantor and Warren Aspinall, it seemed as though Arsenal were still wallowing in their defeat against Crystal Palace on Monday night.

Brighton were much the better team for the first 70 minutes with the goals from Trossard and Mwepu being the icing on the cake. Some of the football played watching the extended highlights back was fantastic.

We still needed some luck when Gabriel Martinelli had his header ruled out for offside and Arsenal hit the bar twice.

Robert Sanchez also made a couple of fantastic saves in the final 10 minutes as the Gunners tried to fight back.

It was nail-biting stuff, not helped by six minutes of injury time. Six minutes! I kept thinking that any second now, Arsenal would equalise.

The leveller never came however, and Brighton took the three points to move up to 11th spot in the Premier League.

As for the Gunners, two defeats in a row is not good for their Champions League hopes. Maybe they are at the start of a bad spell just as the Albion are hopefully now coming out of? It happens to most teams at some point in the season.

I was so enthralled by the end of the football that I almost forgot to turn off the radio and the television on for the Grand National.

The dog seemed quite pleased when we made the change as he had been going wild whilst I was jumping for joy at the full-time whistle. None of this impressed Mrs Noble as her family are all lifelong Gooners.

The wife's mood was at least to be lifted by what happened as the runners approached the start line in the National. The famous words "And they're off!" set the horses off on a sunny and dry afternoon in Liverpool.

As they went over the Melling Road, it was "Over to you John Hamner." I remember that saying from years ago.

Rarely since have I been so excited by the National as I was when they approached the last fence and Noble Yeats was looking like he could win.

The noise in the house was almost as loud as at Aintree and to my utter amazement, Noble Yeats took first place. A load of dosh was coming my way, which of course means another trip to the Amex Superstore soon.

In an immediate response to Noble Yeats winning, I quickly loaded up the National Lottery App and fired in five lucky dips. Unfortunately, I crashed and burned at that point with a harsh reminder of why I am rarely a gambling man.

It would be rude not to put a couple of quid on a draw at Spurs next week though, right…

Just like my washing, Spurs were hung out to dry
April 16th 2022

Spurs 0 Brighton 1

Just like the previous Saturday when the sun shone and blue skies showed their face as Brighton won at Arsenal, it was a glorious afternoon weather-wise for the trip to North London's other club, Spurs

So nice was it in fact that I washed and put on the washing line all my Brighton shirts. They were not the only things hung out to dry; Spurs were too, their good run of form coming to an end against an Albion side making it two wins from two in our capital city in the space of seven days.

Spurs have a cockerel on their badge, but they did not live up to the famous saying of being the "Cock of the Walk". They did certainly did not dominate, failing to have a shot on target for the whole game as it finished Spurs 0-1 Brighton.

When you think about how they have controlled games and scored goals for fun over recent weeks, it is extraordinary that Brighton were able to prevent Robert Sanchez from needing to make save.

The planning and preparation that went into blocking out both Son Heung-min and Harry Kane was spot on from Graham Potter. The players carried out our managerial maestro's tactics brilliantly to complete another memorable victory.

Audere est Facere (to dare is to do) is the Spurs motto. Brighton reversed it with a daring performance in what was a tough match.

I also did something daring – no, not another bet on my new Ladbrokes app – by inviting a Tottenham-supporting friend around to watch the game with me, having paid for a BT Sports subscription to witness the action.

He thought that Spurs' recent form would carry them to victory. That and lightning never striking twice. Brighton had already used up their quota of wins in North London in beating Arsenal 2-1, right?

Wrong. He was gobsmacked when in the 90th minute, Leandro Trossard slotted one home with the outside of his right foot.

My settee springs took one of their biggest bashings of the season and why not? Once the six minutes of injury time were successfully ridden out, this was one of Brighton's best wins so far.

My friend was gracious in defeat. He had said how badly Spurs were playing, but as the game went on that changed to the realisation that Brighton were playing so well as to make Tottenham look poor. A Spurs supporter saying how good the Albion are. Now that is what we like to hear!

Brighton were relentless throughout the 90 minutes, running their socks off and closing down any Spurs advances. That helped to silence the home crowd.

The official attendance was announced as being 58,685, but the Spurs supporters were eerily quiet. It was the three thousand Brighton fans making all the noise, singing their hearts out and making us all watching from home proud.

Antonio Conte seemed to have decided that Brighton's most dangerous player was Enock Mwepu. Spurs appeared to be out to get Mwepu one way or another, eventually leading to him picking up a yellow card.

Potter had to make an important decision at half time, taking Mwepu off to ensure that the Albion did not drop to 10 men in the second half.

There were six bookings in the 90 minutes, three per team. Referee Craig Pawson managed to not see a clear red card however, when Marc Cucurella was elbowed in the face by Dejan Kulusevski. He clearly looked angry about being out played so many times by Cucurella!

In my last two pieces, I predicted that Brighton would do things the hard way. Of course, not beating Norwich was always going to set us up for wins at Arsenal and Spurs.

Both victories serve as a reminder that we do have a great squad and a tactical coach who can teach these players and get the best from them.

The Albion are now just one point off their highest ever total in the Premier League. They will certainly exceed 41 and may even equal it with a draw at Manchester City in midweek.

Then, it is back to the Amex to face Southampton at home. If the football against the Saints can match what we have seen in North London these past few weeks, then we will be in for a treat. Up the Albion!

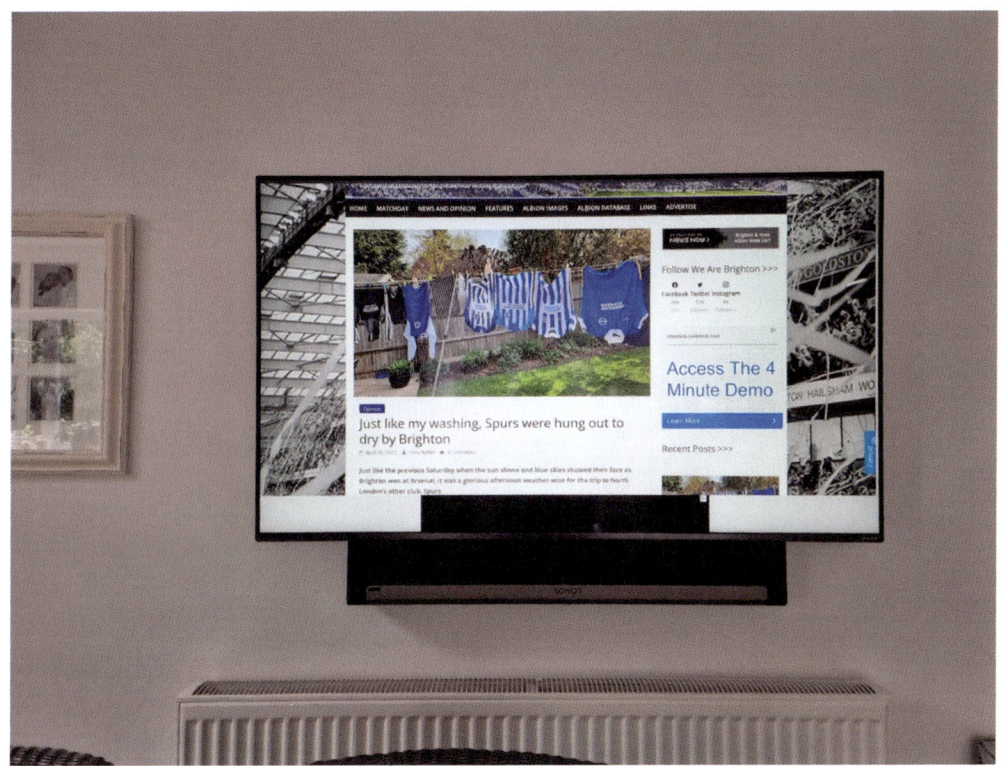

Seeing Your Article Hung Out To Dry On The Big Screen

Brighton can be proud it took Rick O'Shea to win it for Man City
April 23rd 2022

Man City 3 Brighton 0

As I waited patiently for Johnny Cantor on BBC Radio Sussex to tell us that Brighton had kicked off against Manchester City, Arsenal were already a goal ahead against Chelsea on the TV.

The Gunners taking an early lead against their London rivals came as a bit of a shock. Maybe there would be hope for the Albion at the Etihad Stadium?

Playing City is always a strange experience. I was confident that Brighton would be doing their utmost to try and at least get a point.

And yet everyone knew if City turned up at their best then they would still win, no matter how well the Albion played.

What made this game doubly difficult was how important it was for the home team. They had to win to retake their throne at the top of the Premier League by one point from Liverpool. As we all know, City eventually did this convincingly in the second half.

In the first half, Brighton did everyone that could be asked of them in keeping the ball out of the Albion net.

One highlight was some exceptional defending from Moises Caicedo which prevented a goal following a wayward clearance by Robert Sanchez. All of the other attempts City had were thankfully wide of the post.

Graham Potter had said before the game that Brighton were facing the best team in the world. He, the players and us fans could all be happy then to go into half time with the score at 0-0.

Little did we know that City would bring out their new star signing in the second half and play with 12 men. The new addition was Rick O'Shea!

The first Man City goal came in the 53rd minute. Riyad Mahrez took a shot which took a Rick O'Shea off Joel Veltman to beat Robert Sanchez.

This was then then followed by Phil Foden having a go from distance. Again, Rick O'Shea got involved to deflect the ball off Enock Mwepu.

City now led 2-0 though two goals which Brighton could put down to pure bad luck. There were still 25 minutes left but it was a big hill for the Albion to climb and suddenly, their passing became unusually inaccurate.

There were not many chances for Brighton and the game was well and truly up when City made the most of another misplaced clearance by Sanchez.

Oleksandr Zinchenko intercepted and played the ball through to Bernardo Silva who buried the chance into the back of the net. Man City 3-0 Brighton and that is how it ended.

From listening on the radio, you got the feeling that the Albion continued to fight but they just could not match the quality of the league leaders – especially that Rick O'Shea chap.

Defeat at the Etihad Stadium should not take away from two excellent recent away performances, however. Wins at Arsenal and Spurs leave Brighton on 40 points and in 10th place.

We will beat our all-time record of 41 points and who knows, we might win at the Amex this Sunday against Southampton. Bring it on.

Finally, folks, the Albion are in the process of setting up a brand-new Fan Advisory Board. I was informed last week that I have made the shortlist and the club website will soon show the applicants vying for your votes.

I am asking now for your support. Please give me your vote via the website when it appears online next week. Thanks in advance – and up the Albion!

Brighton give us a goal at last, but not a wave from the team coach
April 23rd 2022

Brighton 2 Southampton 2

What could be better than travelling down to the Amex on a sunny Sunday lunchtime? Brighton had performed much better on the road in their past three matches, so would this form continue at home and lead to us home fans finally seeing a goal?

It had been over 90 days since Adam Webster last gave us something to celebrate when he scored against Chelsea. Arriving at the ground early, Southampton fans were heard to be saying they did not hold out much hope for their chances against the Albion.

I took my friend along with me who is a Tottenham Hotspur supporter. We sampled the fish and chips outside the ground and very good they were too.

My guest was soon singing the praises of the Amex Stadium and how great it looked. I said to him: "It always looks great, especially when the sun shines and the Albion win!" We have enjoyed plenty of sun this season, but not quite as many wins.

Whilst we were enjoying our fish and chips, the Brighton team coach drove past the Seagulls Superstore area. As it made its way slowly through the crowd, I spotted Graham Potter at the front.

Both me and an Albion supporter much younger than me who I was stood next to waved at Graham. This little chap was frantic, sending all the players sat on the bus the best of luck.

The players seemed to think that because the coach had blacked out windows, fans outside cannot see them and so they did not need to wave back.

Well, just to let them know, we can see you lads when the light shines right on the coach as it was on this afternoon.

Not one of the players sitting on the left side of the coach acknowledged the fans. I felt sorry for the young man, it seemed like a hello from an Albion hero would have made his day!

Waves may have been in short supply, but it did not take long for Brighton to give us a goal and break that scoring duck. It took just two minutes for Danny Welbeck to put the ball in the Southampton net.

Great teamwork in front of the East Stand led to the goal, which looked like would set us up for a winning afternoon.

Taking an early lead gave the players confidence and they were full-on throughout the first half, playing as if they were fighting to stay in the Premier League like Burnley.

Southampton came back with a shot from Tino Livramento which hit the post of Robert Sanchez's goal. The ball bounced off the woodwork, hit Sanchez in the back and then Che Adams nearly connected with it. Thank goodness he didn't as Adams had an empty goal to aim at.

Adam Webster was a picture of calm in the first half, and it was great to see him back in the side, moving the ball up the field so well.

Welbeck too was playing well, and he had a shot which hit Fraser Forster and went out for a corner. More good build up play from an Enock Mwepu chip had created that chance.

Neal Maupay had my Spurs friend and me out of our seats when he appeared to have doubled the advantage, all of us in the East Upper monetarily forgetting about the offside rule.

Another bagatelle-type moment in the Saints box followed but Maupay could not quite force it over the line. Brighton had scored once, was it greedy of to expect another?

No, it wasn't. Webster found Welbeck, who cut inside and crossed to Trossard. Trossard tried to return to Welbeck, only for Mohammed Salisu to intercept the pass.

Unfortunately for Mr Salisu, his rushing back saw him Rick O'Shea it into the back of the net to make it 2-0 with 44 minutes played.

Having seen Rick O'Shea score twice when Man City beat Brighton 3-0 on Wednesday night, it was good of him to make an emergency transfer to the Albion and give us the luck we have been missing in recent months.

Five minutes of first half injury time were needed after Livramento had been stretchered off. It has since been reported that Livramento suffered a bad knee injury and faces many weeks out.

We wish him well for his recovery from such an unfortunate injury. It was no foul, Livramento just landed badly after jumping for the ball.

With 60 seconds of the additional time to go, Marc Cucurella challenged Nathan Tella and the Saints player went down just outside the penalty area.

Southampton now had a free kick in James Ward-Prowse territory. I have seen Ward-Prowse score so many times from this position that I guaranteed my friend it was about to become Brighton 2-1 Southampton.

As sure as eggs are eggs, Ward-Prowse bent the ball into the left-hand corner. Everyone knows how brilliant he is when taking free kicks and yet here we were, awestruck again.

My next pearl of wisdom to my Spurs supporting friend was that this may not now be plain sailing for Brighton. Little did I expect the Albion to lose the plot slightly in a second half which could have gone either way, as Potter said in his press conference after the match.

Brighton kicked towards the North Stand and needed a third goal to put pressure back on Southampton. It was the Saints who scored next however, an Oriel Romeu backheel placing the ball perfectly into the feet of Ward-Prowse. He fired another unstoppable shot to make it all-square at Brighton 2-2 Southampton.

Sanchez had to show his best when springing like a cat to save a shot from Shane Long which looked like it was going in. Things became very bitty from end-to-end with Southampton appearing to be the most likely scorers of the next goal.

Almost from nowhere, a neat piece of play enabled Pascal Gross to slam a shot past Forster and into the back of the net.

Sadly, it turned out to be fractionally offside once VAR at Stockley Park had drawn their lines, by no more than a fingertip.

Four times we had been out of our seats celebrating goals over the 90 minutes. Two counted and two did not, but the fact Albion fans were getting so much exercise jumping up and down made this an improvement on the last few home games.

The hard work and effort put in by the squad paid off with another point added to the tally, helping us equal our best Premier League total of 41.

Even a draw from the trip to face Wolves at Molineux next weekend will break the record. Surely a reason for the players to wave out the coach window to the kids and us old boy's next time.

One last thing before I sign off – please remember to vote for me via the Albion website for the new Fan Advisory Board. The voting is meant to go live this week. Thank you in advance – and up the Albion!

WHO'S NEXT?

That winning feeling from the driver's seat to Cornwall
April 30th 2022

Wolves 0 Brighton 3

Whilst Brighton went to Wolves in search of a result to surpass their all-time Premier League points high of 41, I was busy driving from Sussex to Cornwall for a week in the west country.

This was not an ideal way to concentrate on the game, even as the Albion audio commentary coming through painted a really good picture of what was going at Molineux whilst we weaved our way through the back roads to the seaside village of Downderry.

Something which I had forgotten about until the Albion's goals started raining in was the delay in the commentary, whereby my watch notifies me of goings on about a minute before the audio caught up.

It was a busy afternoon in that regard, the watch going beep beep beep, followed shortly afterwards by Johnny Cantor and Warren Aspinall leaping out of their commentary positions with excitement.

Brighton put three goals past Wolves and kept a clean sheet to shoot up to ninth in the Premier League. It certainly made the long drive more enjoyable, and of course we now sit on a record points tally with a further nine up for grabs in the final three matches of the season.

I was expecting Wolves to give us a real test having lost their past two matches. They never got the chance to do that; according to Johnny and Warren, this was the best football of the season played by the Albion.

Watching the extended highlights from Wolves 0-3 Brighton back once we arrived in Cornwall, it was clear that the assessment on the radio was right.

From the moment Enock Mwepu fired an early shot off from about 30 yards which put Wolves goalkeeper Jose Sa at full stretch to save, the Albion were brilliant.

Mwepu had a second shot which again kept Sa on his toes. Wolves' Joao Moutinho saw a rare Wolves effort deflected by a Brighton defender before the first major talking point arrived.

Solly March moved swiftly down the right, beat his defender, and delivered a cross followed by appeals for handball against Romain Saiss.

VAR checked and because Saiss' arm position did not appear natural, referee Simon Hooper pointed to the penalty spot after watching the incident back on the pitch side monitor.

Up stepped Alexis Mac Allister. Suddenly, it dawned on me that my watch had not buzzed for a goal as the radio commentary was about to describe the penalty.

So, when Johnny told us that Mac Allister had hit the post, it did not come as a surprise. I felt sad for Mac Allister as he has been playing so well over the past few weeks and missed penalties can have an impact on players.

Little did we know that there would be a quick chance to put things right. A foul on Moises Caicedo led to a free kick inside the Brighton half. Lewis Dunk took it swiftly, dropping the ball over the top for Danny Welbeck to collect.

Welbeck was swiftly brought to the ground by Willy Boly and Brighton had a second penalty in the space of nine minutes. To the surprise of many, Mac Allister stepped up again to take.

He placed a powerful shot to the same side as his first effort, only this time it was inside the post. Sa got a hand to it but could not keep the ball out because of how hard Mac Allister had hit it.

It showed great bravery for Mac Allister to have another go from the spot having missed that first penalty. He has a top mentality and that is why he has become one of the Albion's most important players.

Brighton scored their second on 70 minutes when a series of moves put Welbeck into a position to lay off to Trossard, who made no mistake with a shot past Sa into the far corner.

The football in the build up to that goal was different class, cutting apart a Wolves defence who do not normally concede many goals.

Boly had Wolves' only shot on target next, a header from a well-placed corner which found the safe hands of Robert Sanchez. The Albion goalkeeper made it look so easy.

Brighton added a deserved third with five minutes left to play. The move was started by Trossard getting wiped out, although referee Mr Hooper played a good advantage.

Marc Cucurella found himself with the chance to cross. The ball was headed clear by a Wolves defender but only as far as Yves Bissouma, who swiftly moved onto his right foot and struck a low shot which hit the back of the net from outside the penalty area.

Wolves hit the left-hand post through Pedro Neto with the final kick of the game. That piece of luck was deserved by Brighton, who had played well enough to earn the clean sheet and a three-goal margin of victory.

Those Albion fans who made the journey must have enjoyed their day. It certainly sounded like it, the away supporters being heard loud and clear over the airwaves.

The noise our fans generate on the road is always louder than what we can manage at the Amex. Perhaps that is why we have such a poor home record?

Maybe we need a couple of chanting managers in the East and West Stands to get the entire stadium working in conjunction with the North?

Saturday evening games do tend to have a better atmosphere and that is where we head next, a 5:30pm kick off for the visit of Manchester United.

The late start means that we can get back to Sussex from Cornwall for the game, even if it will involve a 7am departure. There will be no radio commentary or watch alerts to keep me company for the return journey.

Instead, it will be back to watching the Albion live – and I fancy us to beat United too on our way to claiming nine points over the next three matches. Up the Albion!

Once last thing – can I ask for your support in the elections for the Albion Fan Advisory Board? I am listed as Anthony Noble and if voted onto the board, I will do my utmost to put forward all fan ideas and suggestions. Thanks in advance.

CR 7 Museum in Madeira

An evening football unlikely to feature in Cristiano Ronaldo Museum
May 7th 2022

Brighton 4 Man Utd 0

Before Saturday night, I had only ever seen a chocolate Cristiano Ronaldo before. That was on holiday to his home island of Madeira, in the amazing Ronaldo Museum.

Spread over two floors, it contains glass cabinets full of all the trophies he has won in his along with all his memorabilia. My God, he has won some medals.

It seems unlikely that what we saw at the Amex when Ronaldo and Manchester United paid a visit will ever feature in the museum. One of the world's great ever footballers was part of a team beaten 4-0 as Brighton put in another wonderful performance.

I had spent the week on holiday in Cornwall. I was desperate to come back and watch the match, not only to see Ronaldo in the flesh (rather than chocolate) but because I had a feeling that the day might go well for the Albion.

My dear wife said that we could head home early on Friday evening to ensure we did not miss the game. I was so grateful to her and cutting the holiday short by a day obviously paid off by Saturday night when Brighton had an historic 4-0 win against United in the bag.

We left Cornwall at 3pm and were back in Sussex by 7:45pm. The washing went straight into the machine and the suitcases were put away in the loft.

The poor dog did not know what was going on. No sooner had we collected him than he was off again to spend the day with a relative whilst we headed down to the Amex.

Speaking of relatives, I had a message from just after the final whistle. He is a Manchester United supporter and was watching the game on catch up.

He said, and I quote: "I am half an hour behind. Game is so boring, poor quality from both sides." What on earth was he watching? It cannot have been the same game as us.

The football played by Brighton was brilliant. They ran rings around United, controlled the entire game and worked hard for each other. He must have been suffering from a case of sour grapes.

There was a brief shower when we arrived at the Amex and that made the pitch slicker. The surface looked immaculate, and the ground staff must be congratulated on the job they have done this season.

It was not until I did the Amex Stadium Tour in October that I learned the pitch is not flat for a reason; clever stuff really and something you cannot tell until you are level with the grass.

Ronaldo was the centre of attention during the warmups. He practiced a free kick against David De Gea, slowly taking his paces back and then one to the side.

He stepped up and... the ball went miles over the bar. That gave me more confidence that the Albion could get a result, and of course the exact same thing happened when Ronaldo took a free kick in the first half.

Brighton did so well to ensure that was the only chance he had in the entire game. Maybe chocolate Ronaldo would have been more threatening?!

United were in good form coming into the game having beaten Brentford 3-0 on Monday night. Brighton have been playing well too, and we have surpassed our highest ever Premier League points tally with lots of wins and goals coming away from home in recent weeks.

What has been missing is a home performance. Well, we certainly got one on this occasion. From no Amex wins since Boxing Day, only three all season in total and scoring just 12 goals to beating Manchester United 4-0. Talk about a stylish way to break the run!

It took barely 15 minutes for us all to witness the skill and courage of Moises Caicedo. A rebound fell to the feet of Caicedo and he expertly placed a low shot along he ground and into the corner of De Gea's goal.

The Amex erupted and Caicedo ran over the celebrate in front of the East Stand. He was embraced by Yves Bissouma which was great to see and clearly all Caicedo's Albion teammates were so happy for him in scoring his first Premier League goal.

Pascal Gross floated a free kick to Danny Welbeck but his shot went over the crossbar. A 1-0 lead did not feel safe to me as we all know what United are capable of – they can even find a way to score a penalty after the final whistle.

Leandro Trossard had a shot which flew just past De Gea's left post. One of Robert Sanchez's pinpoint long kicks then released Welbeck, but his lob was over the bar as chances for the Albion came thick and fast.

Everything was looking good when we went into half time, but again I had to remind myself that this was Manchester United we were playing. "Come on Tony, you know what they always do in the last minute, do not get too excited yet."

There would be no need to worry as Brighton of course were out of sight by the last minute. They were out of sight by the hour mark actually after one of the best 15 minutes of football ever.

Marc Cucurella scoring the second four minutes into the second half was the greatest moment of the season for me. He has played his socks off and thoroughly deserved to get his first Premier League goal.

Cucurella was emotional and so was I, actually. It is amazing to see a young man from Spain enjoying himself so much in Brighton. I hope he and his family love living in the area as boy, do we need him to stay!

Obviously, the team talk from Ralf Rangnick had no impact. Bruno Fernandes said afterwards "Brighton had more determination than us" and he was spot on.

All United could do in response to the Albion going two ahead was offer Sanchez catching practice. There was nothing he could not handle on this occasion, and he even played a big part in the third Brighton goal.

Another of those kicks more deadly than a sniper shot sent Cucurella away down the left. He found Trossard who dinked to Gross and the German weaved his way through the United defence to slot past De Gea.

The stadium was electric. A fantastic goal starting with Sanchez and ending with Gross. United were being carved apart and it showed on the faces and body language of the visitors.

Less than two minutes later and Brighton were at it again. Gross went aerial to find Welbeck. He popped the ball over De Gea and although Diogo Dalot was covering, Trossard was on hand to help it over the line.

There was a VAR check for handball, but Trossard looked seriously confident that the goal would stand. And it did. Brighton 4-0 Manchester United. Oh my.

United came to life a bit after that, as if they felt "Maybe we should try and get a goal?!" Ronaldo crossed for Edinson Cavani to head, only for Sanchez to pull off what has to be described as a cat-like save.

Alexis Mac Allister charged up the other end and nearly added an unthinkable fifth for Brighton, hitting the post. It was a much more open game now and Sanchez made a world class stop to keep out a Fernandes screamer.

Welbeck then curled one just wide. It was so close that we in the East Stand were convinced it was in, which would have been the cherry on the cake.

The atmosphere throughout the game and at full time was unlike anything I have seen this season. That has to give the squad a boost for the final two games, away at Leeds next Sunday and home to West Ham at the Amex on Sunday 22nd May.

One last thing, if you have not voted in the Fan Advisory Board elections yet then please consider giving me your vote. I am listed as Anthony Noble.

The poll closes on Friday 13th May and if elected, I will be happy to put forward all your ideas and suggestions to the club next season. A chocolate statue of Cucurella, anyone?

Long grass, dry pitch, loud crowd: Brighton earned a good point at Leeds
May 15th 2022

Leeds 1 Brighton 1

Going to Elland Road to face Leeds players fighting for their Premier League existence was never going to be easy for Brighton.

I wondered if the Albion would find it similar to stepping into a gladiatorial arena. More than 34,000 home fans made quite the noise over the BBC Radio Sussex airwaves in a reminder of just what a big club Leeds are.

Leeds had certainly pulled out all the stops to make things even more difficult for Brighton. Johnny Cantor and Warren Aspinall reported that the grass was long and not much water had been sprayed on it before kick-off.

This had been done to go some way towards preventing the Albion playing their normal slick football and it worked to a degree.

Leeds needed to do something to make up for missing two key players through suspension, something that Everton will now experience after they picked up two red cards for reckless tackles in defeat to Brentford.

There is much to play for on the final day of the season with the title, relegation, and some European spots still to be decided.

The sun was shining at Elland Road, and we were also told that Tony Bloom was in attendance, enjoying the weather with his shades in tow.

Leeds came flying out of the traps like greyhounds and Brighton seemed to be caught by surprise, making mistakes in possession.

It took the Albion 10 minutes or so to settle but once they did, they began to control the game despite the pitch not being in their favour.

Solly March had the Albion's first chance, but he scuffed off target the sort of shot you would expect him to normally score.

Three more chances came and went with luck not being on Brighton's side, otherwise they could have put the game to bed in the first half.

Alexis Mac Allister and Leandro Trossard produced some great play to create a close opportunity. Moises Caicedo was on the deck and just failed to get the ball over the line and Pascal Gross followed that up with another near miss.

Not only would a goal give Brighton the lead, but it would also damage Leeds morale and shut up the loud home crowd. Danny Welbeck provided the moment in the 21st minute with a goal brilliantly set up by Yves Bissouma.

The Albion kept having chances. Mac Allister had a header which landed on the roof of the net and he then fired wide after Trossard moved the ball well into a dangerous area.

Leeds came back to finish the first half strongly. They had several corners to up the pressure. One of these attempts led to the first of three brilliant saves from Robert Sanchez, nothing less than superb goalkeeping.

1-0 at half time was not the score that Brighton deserved for their performance. Unfortunately, those missed shots were now history.

I expected Leeds to come out all guns blazing in their battle to avoid relegation, and if they did that then the worry was that Brighton would live to regret not taking at least one of those golden chances.

Raphinha was the man to step up for Leeds under the gorgeous Yorkshire sun. He came close to bringing the game level early in the second half and then had a free kick which Sanchez produced an outstanding save to keep out.

The ball looked certain to go into the top right corner until Sanchez made a cat-like leap to save the day. Years ago, they used to call Peter Bonetti of Chelsea the cat; well, I think that nicknamed needs to be resurrected for our own dynamic goalkeeper.

Marc Cucurella was next to deny Raphinha with a recovery and interception which prevented perhaps another goal. By now, it was starting to sound as if the Albion were hanging on.

They still had a chance to make the game safe though in the final five minutes. Good play down the left resulted in a switch to the right and cross into the box for Welbeck to head home number two. Unfortunately, he headed just wide.

And then Leeds got the goal they needed. Joe Geldhardt just about managed to get the ball over to the back post where Leeds substitute Pascal Struijk nodded in.

Brighton had come within minutes of a 1-0 win and yet had to settle for a point. It just goes to show that in the Premier League, a one-goal lead is never enough, and it is not over until the fat lady sings.

The result meant Leeds climbed out of the relegation zone ahead of the final weekend of the season. Brighton sit 10th with 48 points and one home game left to play against West Ham, where we will see if we can break the 50 points barrier in the Premier League for the first time. It has been an excellent campaign and fingers crossed we can end it on a high. Onwards and upwards and Up the Albion!

There We Are Right Up There !

What a year to have a Brighton season ticket for the first time
May 22nd 2022

Brighton 3 West Ham 1

Having been a Brighton fan since I first went to the Goldstone Ground as a 10-year-old in 1965, this 2021-22 season has been the first time in my life that I have had an Albion season ticket.

I could not have picked a better year to finally join as a season ticket holder, could I? And thanks to the support of WAB, I have been able to share the journey with all of you through my weekly perspective of each game.

Hopefully, you have found it interesting to read about the thoughts and feelings of somebody who until now has never been able to attend home matches regularly.

Away games remain a no-go, so instead I have reported back on all the different efforts I have made to listen, watch, receive text updates and even place a rare sports bet to keep up to date with the Albion on the road.

With the assistance of WAB, I am going to try and put all my pieces together in a book covering the entire 2021-22 season.

It will serve as a reminder of the best season that Brighton have ever had, recall some tremendous games and the sad times we went through. Watch out for it in the coming months.

And so, to West Ham at home, the final day of a memorable season. The form of the last few weeks gave me confidence going into the game that it would be Brighton "forever blowing bubbles" and not Hammers fans come the full-time whistle.

Our visitors from London might have thought otherwise at half time, but a brilliant Brighton effort turned around a 1-0 deficit to win 3-1 thanks to 45 minutes of 120 percent effort.

As many pundits have already written, it was the togetherness of the Albion squad that got them over the line for a fifth win in eight matches.

What a shame that the season has to end now. But hey, the players need a break and as Johnny Cantor said on the final Albion Unlimited podcast of the season, it is only nine weeks until the 2022-23 season kicks off.

With a winter World Cup in Qatar between November and December, it is going to be an even busier year of football than normal in the next campaign.

The Amex once again looked splendid in the late afternoon sun and Brighton fans were in very good voice, as they had been in that unbelievable 4-0 win over Manchester United.

Before the start, there was a presentation for West Ham legend Mark Noble as this was to be his final game ahead of retirement.

As far as I know, I am no relation to Mark even though we share the same surname. Interestingly, my father was born around the corner from the old Boleyn Ground in the East End of London in the 1920s.

His first love as a boy was therefore West Ham, until he moved to Brighton as a young lad. Maybe there is a connection between this Noble and that Noble?

The perfect send off for that Noble would have been a Hammers win to qualify them for the Europa League.

They had everything to play for as our good friend Mr Kevin Friend blew the whistle to signal the start of the game.

Brighton though were not interested in Noble or West Ham's dreams of the Europa League. Alexis Mac Allister made a quick start, finding Marc Cucurella.

His dinked cross towards Moises Caicedo resulted in a shot at goal which was well saved by Lukasz Fabianski.

That set the tone for some good Albion play. Significant build-ups led to goal scoring opportunities, and one could say Brighton were unlucky not to go ahead.

The Albion were the better team until the final five minutes of the half. A shot from Michail Antonio following a coming together with Lewis Dunk rocketed straight into the back of the Brighton net.

It was clear from a replay from a certain angle that Dunk had been pushed by Antonio. Our friend Kevin Friend did not agree though; no free kick, the goal stood, and Brighton went into the break trailing.

I was certain West Ham would look for a hammer blow second goal soon into the second half. To the amazement of most watching, it was actually the Albion who scored within five minutes.

Once again there was nice approach play from Cucurella and Pascal Gross down the left-hand side playing towards the North Stand.

A ball across goal found its way to the back post where Joel Veltman arrived to fire along the floor and past Fabianski, making it 1-1.

One-touch football from Brighton was now starting to open up the West Ham defence. Neal Maupay showed real skill to almost make it 2-1 shortly after the Veltman goal as the team continued to work hard to move ahead.

The teamwork and the style of football played were a credit to Graham Potter and his coaching team, as it has been for much of the season.

Caicedo intercepted again to find Danny Welbeck in a great position. Unfortunately, the angle was just a little too tight and Welbeck curved the wrong side of the post.

Goal number two for the Albion eventually arrived on 80 minutes. Gross produced a turning swivel and fired off a shot with his supposedly weaker foot to beat Fabianski.

The three-quarters of the Amex filled with Brighton fans erupted. What a goal from Gross, his second in as many home matches. Pascal Gross, we want you to stay!

An entertaining final 10 minutes were now in store. West Ham needed to find a way back for the Europa League, the Albion needed to hold on or score another goal to take the three points.

Tariq Lamptey crossed for Welbeck whose header was held by Fabianski. When the board flashed up to show three minutes of injury time, the game still could have gone either way. I was thinking the Hammers would claw one back...

Brighton won the ball in midfield to force a corner in the dying minutes. I was so excited that I cannot remember who took the corner, although I can say with certainty Welbeck met it with a brilliant header to make it Brighton 3-1 West Ham.

The Hammers had been taken apart and the Amex went mad. A wonderful afternoon was rounded off by the players and their families doing a lap of honour around the pitch.

I was quite emotional by the end, seeing the effort the players put in and what it meant to everyone as we all came together to celebrate a record-breaking season.

To those Potter non-believers, Brighton have shown that they are building a great squad and the future looks brighter than ever. Let us just hope we do not need to sell the family silver this summer.

Who will stay and who will go remains to be seen? I do know that I will not be on the Fan Advisory Board as I was not one of the lucky ones elected; but good luck to all the folks who did. I know they will all do us proud over the next two years.

All that remains for me to say is what a roller coaster this season has been. To the Albion, thank you for the entertainment. To everyone else, thank you for reading.

Roll on nine weeks' time when we get to do it all again for my second year as a Brighton season ticket holder.

Tony Noble June 2022

AUTOGRAPHS PAGE

Printed in Great Britain
by Amazon